Providential Promised Provision Provided

by Freda Lindsay

Published by
Christ For The Nations Inc.
P.O. Box 769000
Dallas, TX 75376-9000

Printed 1996
©1996
Christ For The Nations Inc.
All Rights Reserved

All Scripture NKJV unless otherwise noted.

Dedication

To all the friends of Christ For The Nations who invested in this missions ministry that is working in 120 countries, has built nearly 10,000 Native Churches, supplied 50 million pieces of free gospel literature, helped raise up 30 Bible schools in Mexico, Canada, Belarus, Germany, Bulgaria, Chile, Romania, Argentina, Peru, Sri Lanka, India, Thailand, South Africa, Singapore, Jamaica, Zimbabwe, Zambia, Nigeria, Nagaland, Japan, etc. and furnished food, clothing and medical supplies to the poor, the refugees and to disaster areas.

Acknowledgment

Our deepest appreciation to the dedicated employees of Christ For The Nations, some of whom have labored faithfully with us for over a quarter of a century.

To the Board and Advisory Council who have walked with us and helped to guide us.

To the over 25,000 students who have attended CFNI over the years, coming from virtually every nation, often at great sacrifice to their parents, their families and themselves.

To my own diligent secretary, Denise Allen, who has assisted me in many ways to make this book possible.

And to Patti Conn, our Managing Editor, who has personally guided this book through its entire printing.

Foreword

I can't tell you how much it means to have a mother-in-law like Freda Lindsay. Right from the start, she welcomed me into the family with open arms. And so many times since then, she has gone out of her way to make me feel special. There's a special place in my heart just for her!

Her whole family sees her as more than a mom, mother-in-law, or grandmother. Several years ago, my daughter, Marcy, wrote the following article for a school paper, sharing her feelings about her very special grandmother.

Shirley Lindsay

**A TRIBUTE TO FREDA LINDSAY
by her 16-year-old granddaughter, Marcy Lindsay,
for her sophomore term paper in 1994.**

"Takeoff will be in five minutes. Please fasten your seat belts, lift your seats to an upright position and put up your trays. The 'No Smoking' sign has been turned on."

This is a familiar sound to my grandmother, Freda Lindsay. Just thinking of her, a plane appears in my mind. She is constantly traveling from one place to another. She flies to mission fields, banquets, conventions, funerals and wherever God points her. It seems like it would be dreary and boring, but she looks at it like it is a thrill and a way to keep her occupied after the death of her husband, whom she loved dearly.

Sometimes my parents are not able to tell me where in the world she is and that is just not an expression. Wherever she goes, she is always collecting souvenirs. Our house is filled with memories of her, and I cannot imagine it without them. When I see them, I think of her traveling in foreign countries, not being able to speak the languages and people coming up to her, only looking at her outward appearance, and not knowing what they are getting themselves into, with her demanding power to get what she wants and nothing less.

Wherever she goes, she is known by many. When I went with her to Israel, where she has one of her yearly tours, I could see we were treated well only because she was there. We would receive things for free, where others would pay a bundle. People were so kind and giving. They even gave us cheaper rates on hotels and buses.

One time my grandmother was on a plane and they were going to crash. She prayed, stayed calm, and did what she was told to do. A few moments later, the plane was flying back on track with no problems. It looked as though nothing were ever wrong. And if that was not enough, a lady my grandmother did not know was on the plane, and she approached my grandmother with the assurance that the plane would not crash with my grandmother on it.

Even though she spends plenty of time on planes, her work is what is so important. One of her main goals is trying to get people baptized with the Holy Spirit.

Thousands have been baptized with the Holy Spirit because of her teachings and blessings among them. She is the type of person that when you hear her speak, you are touched in more than one way. She makes you feel good inside, and yet she can still get the point across.

She is an excellent role model. When things get rough, she gets tough. When her husband, founder of Christ For The Nations Institute, died, she took over. She is also over Bible schools all over the world, including: Germany, Canada, Jamaica, Argentina, Romania, Nigeria, Bulgaria and Belarus. She has also been instrumental in helping build thousands of Native Churches around the world. When she gets going, nothing can stop her.

Not only does she have character, but her honesty is overwhelming. So many have gone astray from God when they become wealthy or famous, but not my grandmother. She does not care who knows her name nor how much money is in her bank account. She is just happy at what she does. One time she was investigated by the authorities. When it was over they could find no fault in her, exactly like Daniel. They even stated she was the only one they had ever investigated that actually gave all money where it had been designated. Those are facts that show the integrity of Freda Lindsay.

Looking at her life, it is clearly seen that she loves the Lord, she is known by many, she is a woman of integrity, and she is most likely found on a plane. Overall, she will never be forgotten.

Table of Contents

Introduction 11
Chapter One
    At the Right Time 13
Chapter Two
    Prophecies: True and False 15
Chapter Three
    Refugees — Always Room for One More 17
Chapter Four
    Fasting 20
Chapter Five
    Worship — One of CFNI's Trademarks 22
Chapter Six
    Hitler Builds a Bible School 24
Chapter Seven
    Berlin Wall 33
Chapter Eight
    When Bombs Are Falling 34
Chapter Nine
    In Israel for Rabin's Funeral 37
Chapter Ten
    The Desert Blossoms 43
Chapter Eleven
    Songs in the Night 45
Chapter Twelve
    The First Proclaimed Atheist Nation 47

Chapter Thirteen
  Synagogue Reaches Thousands for Jesus 51
Chapter Fourteen
  God Chooses a Prison 54
Chapter Fifteen
  We Found God's Plan in a Dark Nation 56
Chapter Sixteen
  Vail 58
Chapter Seventeen
  We Need New Furniture 62
Chapter Eighteen
  Above and Beyond 64
Chapter Nineteen
  Extinguished the Raging Fire 68
Chapter Twenty
  Lost and Found 70
Chapter Twenty-One
  Making Choices 72
Chapter Twenty-Two
  Marriages Made in Heaven 74
Chapter Twenty-Three
  A CFNI Match 76
Chapter Twenty-Four
  A Godly Man is Elected 77
Chapter Twenty-Five
  The Grand Finale! 87
Chapter Twenty-Six
  Lacking One Detail 89
Chapter Twenty-Seven
  Spared! 93

Chapter Twenty-Eight
"He Calms the Storms" 95
Chapter Twenty-Nine
The Writer 97
Chapter Thirty
A Change of the Guard 100
Chapter Thirty-One
Our Alumni 102
Chapter Thirty-Two
Reaching the Top 107
Chapter Thirty-Three
Praying for the Pope 109
Chapter Thirty-Four
CFNI Pastors 111
Chapter Thirty-Five
A Heartbreak! A Family Redirected 116
Chapter Thirty-Six
Dogsledding 119
Chapter Thirty-Seven
Khartoum, Sudan Trip 122
Chapter Thirty-Eight
The "Laughing Revival" 127
Chapter Thirty-Nine
Our Greatest Financial Miracle 131
Chapter Forty
A Millionaire Phones Me 134
Chapter Forty-One
From Death to Life 138
Chapter Forty-Two
Friends Indeed 140

Chapter Forty-Three
  A Genuine Missionary 143
Chapter Forty-Four
  Who Despised the Day of Small Things? 145
Chapter Forty-Five
  The Right Employee 148
Chapter Forty-Six
  Not Everybody Likes Me 152
Chapter Forty-Seven
  Honors Galore! 155
Chapter Forty-Eight
  A 55-Year-Long Prayer 159
Chapter Forty-Nine
  Crossing Over 162
Chapter Fifty
  My Greatest Joy 164

Introduction

Over a decade had passed since I wrote *Freda*, my second autobiographical book. By now, the number of miracles had escalated and were piled one on top of the other.

Staff, students, friends and family members were asking, "Isn't it about time you wrote that next book?"

But with the multitudes of manuscripts produced monthly, was one more necessary? Besides, writing a book is hard, intense work.

However, as time passed, I began to consider the new book. After several months of contemplation, I felt I had the "go ahead" signal. Yes, I'd tell about the heaps of miracles. I resolved also to add what really happens: life interspersed with plenty of pressure and problems. But thank God, I have learned to say, "This, too, shall pass."

So, if my true story can help some individual make it through life in victory, my efforts will have been well worth the time.

"In the world you have tribulation *and* trials *and* distress *and* frustration; but be of good cheer — take courage, be confident, certain, undaunted — for I have overcome the world. — I have deprived it of power to harm, have conquered it [for you]" (Jn. 16:33 AMP.).

My life is but another proof that though both triumphs and tragedies come our way, our life can be fulfilling every step of the way.

Chapter One

At the Right Time

Dr. Steve King, a psychiatrist, and his wife, Judy, a therapist, took a leave of absence for a year to study the Bible at CFNI so they could have better results in counseling their clients. They lived on campus in the same dormitory complex where Gordon and I lived for a year after we had sold our home and given the funds to Christ For The Nations Institute.

The Kings were in our Sunday afternoon service the day Gordon, my husband, died of a heart attack on the platform. Dr. King hurried to give him mouth-to-mouth resuscitation. He later told me he did it partially for my benefit, for as soon as he checked Gordon for a pulse, he knew he was dead.

The shock of losing Gordon so quickly, along with the tremendous financial burden we were under at that time, nearly overwhelmed me. We had just purchased seven apartment buildings adjacent to one another, and we owed nearly 100% on all but one of them. We had three years yet to pay on our headquarters building; we owed $450,000 on our auditorium under construction and needed another $300,000 to finish it; several hundred Native Churches were being built overseas; the monthly magazine and books we printed had to be funded; and we were $17,000 overdrawn at the bank — as I learned on the Monday morning after Gordon died. Not one red cent of operating capital did we have!

When four days later our 10-man board voted for me to succeed Gordon, I found myself unable to sleep. So I asked Steve and Judy to pray with me, and requested that Dr. King prescribe sleeping pills for me. After a time of reflection he said, "No, I can't do that for you. If I do, with all you have on your shoulders now, you could easily become addicted. You are going to have to become really strong, and God has already promised you, 'As your days, *so shall* your strength *be*' (Deut. 33:25). Judy and I will pray each day for you, and if you need us at any time day or night, call us."

I shall never forget that wise counsel, which I followed. When their year at CFNI was over, the Kings returned to their practice. Steve said by using God's Word, his counseling so greatly improved, and the results with his clients were so obvious, that he received several promotions.

Since then, Dr. and Mrs. King have traveled overseas to hold doctors' clinics, giving them a great opportunity to share the Word and to lead the physicians to Christ.

"You will show me the path of life; in Your presence *is* fullness of joy; at Your right hand *are* pleasures forevermore" (Psa. 16:11).

Chapter Two

Prophecies: True and False

In Charismatic circles, those in leadership often have prophecies given to them. I'm sure I must have received hundreds of them — written or orally — in my lifetime. I never try to *make* a prophecy come to pass. If it is of God, it will come to pass; if it isn't, I'll leave that to Him.

The Bible does say, "Do not despise prophecies" (I Thes. 5:20). But it also says, "Beloved, do not believe every spirit, but test the spirits, whether they are of God; because many false prophets have gone out into the world" (I Jn. 4:1). Before Christ's ascension to His Father, several times He warned His disciples to, "not be deceived" (Lk. 21:8).

If I had tried to run my life by the many prophecies given to me, I would be in total confusion. Too often, I've seen those who were guided by a "prophecy" make financial or marriage decisions that led them completely out of the will of God. How sad! I believe that sometimes a "prophecy" is just a person's individual desire for the recipient. The one prophesying is not "false" in the sense that he is demonic or evil, he is merely expressing his thoughts or wishes.

I've seen ministers give "wholesale prophecies," going right down a line of people, and each one becoming more "amazing" than the one before! I always wonder, how many of those lives will be completely misguided. The Lord gave us His Holy Spirit to guide us, and we must not depend on "prophecies" alone.

In 1990, a letter came to my office saying that four women were going to die by a certain date that summer. As my secretary read it aloud, I kept on with my work. But when she said, "You're one of the four!" I stopped and listened.

The first one mentioned was evangelist Paul Cain's mother. Now with the law of averages working for me, I could have "prophesied" that one. His mother, age 104, was in the hospital and had been in a coma for two weeks. Yes, she did die a few days later.

My secretary cautioned, "I know the man who gave that prophecy. He's a real man of God." I replied, "I always stay ready, so I have no fear."

Did I walk in fear until that date arrived? Not at all. That date came and went and nothing happened to me. Six years have passed, and God has allowed me to live and continue His work. To Him be the glory!

When I met the evangelist-grandson of one of the other "victims" after the death date predicted, he told me his grandmother was still strong and busy teaching the Word. The fourth person I didn't know personally, nor have I had any information concerning her.

"With long life I will satisfy him, and show him My salvation" (Psa. 91:16).

Chapter Three

Refugees — Always Room for One More

When my father had earned enough money from his grain crop on our homestead in Saskatchewan, Canada, we moved out of the sod house. Father had built a big 10-room house for our large family. Never did neighbors, visitors or newcomers arrive at our door but what Dad took them in, offered them food and a room in which to stay, even if my brothers had to sleep on the hay in the barn.

When we later moved to Portland, Oregon, my dad rented a huge house. I recall one period of time in which not only our family lived there, but also my grandparents and their grown daughter, a married son with his family of three, and a step-uncle. We all shared one narrow bathroom with its tub and commode — thankful for the improvement over the outhouse we had to use when living on the farm.

So it was easy for me in the '80s to invite fleeing refugees from communist countries to our campus for food, housing, clothing and to study God's Word. Once the word was circulated that one of the two families of the Siberian Seven had taken refuge on our campus, other refugees began to arrive steadily. They would escape from their countries by swimming rivers (sometimes with guards shooting at them), climbing mountains, or walking for days to get to a neutral nation.

Aurel, from Romania, was a young man who had risked all, even leaving behind his wife and seven children. An engineer by trade, he immediately found employment. It took two full years before his wife and children were allowed to join him in Dallas. Some sixty of our students welcomed the family at the airport. It was a moving experience to watch the reunion of this father with his family. Today, Aurel has a splendid job, built his own nice home and is actively involved in the local Romanian church.

Once, a fast Russian speed-skater, who was in the United States with his team, came to us secretly wanting help to defect and asking for a sport's scholarship. We told him we had no professional sport's teams and could give no sport's scholarships since ours is strictly a Bible school. He left after counsel and prayer.

Maria and John lived in Romania with four small children. Twice John had attempted escape, but he was caught and imprisoned for a time. Maria then had to look to other family members for food. Realizing that if John were caught trying to leave a third time, his next stay in prison would be long — maybe forever, Maria decided it was her turn. Without consulting anyone, she kissed her four children "goodbye" as they left for school one morning. Together with two friends of hers who were also desiring to escape, Maria left. After the trio had walked for several hours, she phoned a relative to tell him what she was doing, and asked him to please help John with the children.

Praying constantly as they walked for a couple of days, the three made it into a neighboring country. They were immediately taken to a crowded refugee camp, where dozens often slept in a single room.

When news came to us of Maria's plight, we made every effort to secure permission for her to come to our campus — praying, writing letters, calling embassies, appearing on TV and radio programs. Finally, Maria arrived on campus, glad to be here, but longing for her family.

We again went to work — this time to help reunite the family. Again, there was an endless chain of bureaucracy to wade through. But nine months later, John and the four children arrived on campus. It had been eighteen long months since Maria had seen John and the children! One hundred and fifty of our students greeted them at the airport at midnight. It was another emotional moment. The family still lives on campus, and John is one of CFN's faithful employees.

So the refugees have come — from Poland, Hungary, Estonia, Czechoslovakia, Romania, Russia, Uganda, Egypt, Iran, Syria, China and other nations of the world. In some cases, we have to teach them English so they can understand our teachers. It has been a wonderful learning experience for our students, staff and faculty who receive with open arms the 200 internationals who show up at our doorstep each semester to study the Word through our anointed faculty. Also, no doubt it has influenced many of our students to participate in outreaches to foreign lands to take the Gospel to those who have never heard.

Chapter Four

Fasting

In my nearly 60 years of keeping daily diaries, again and again I find one word: "Fasting."

What is the significance of fasting? Isaiah 58:6-9,11,14 gives us the answer: "Is this not the fast that I have chosen: To loose the bonds of wickedness, to undo the heavy burdens, to let the oppressed go free, ... (to) break every yoke? ... That you bring to your house the poor who are cast out; when you see the naked, that you cover him? ... Then your light shall break forth like the morning, your healing shall spring forth speedily, and your righteousness shall go before you; the glory of the LORD shall be your rear guard (your protection). Then you shall call, and the LORD will answer; you shall cry, and He will say, 'Here I am.' ... The LORD will guide you continually, and satisfy your soul in drought, and strengthen your bones. ... Then you shall delight yourself in the LORD."

Do you know anyone who needs to pray and fast for the above reasons? When Jesus' disciples could not cast the demon out of the epileptic boy, He told them, "This kind does not go out except by prayer and fasting" (Matt. 17:21). Jesus cast out the demon and the boy was immediately healed. In fact, Jesus did not say to the disciples, "*If* you fast;" instead He said, "*When* you fast" (Matt. 6:16).

In every believer's life, there will come times when fasting becomes necessary to break satanic strongholds. That's why at Christ For The Nations Institute we set aside one, two or three days each semester for fasting and prayer, dismissing regular classes. The fasting is not compulsory, but virtually every student participates in obedience to God.

My late husband, Gordon, was the most consistent man of prayer I have ever met. He often fasted and prayed, and at times, I would join him on a short fast. Once, he fasted for 30 days for our daughter, Shira, who was compromising in her walk with God. She has now been serving the Lord in Israel for 28 years, and has become an example of one who fasts and prays. She and her husband, Ari, have experienced some very remarkable answers from God as they have prayed and fasted.

Our students, too, often report victories after fasting. One such example was Marty Nystrom, who came to CFNI one summer discouraged and with a real hunger to know God intimately. Unbeknown even to his dean, he went on a 20-day fast. It was then he wrote the song *As the Deer* — a song that has been sung the world over, blessing millions. To God be the glory!

Chapter Five

Worship — One of CFNI's Trademarks

If Christ For The Nations Institute is known for one important characteristic other than its emphasis on the Word and prayer, it's our powerful praise and worship.

When Gordon and I pastored, we quickly learned the importance of music, not only for those in the church, but also as a tremendous tool to attract young people for Christ. So when we started CFNI, we placed a real emphasis on music. And the one outcome that developed early on was that each spring our worship leader and students would produce a cassette of favorite choruses and songs from that year. The demand for these annual productions increased with every new tape, until now many hundreds of thousands have gone worldwide, and the choruses have been translated into scores of languages.

Our anointed chorus tapes inspired others to produce music tapes. For example, a Japanese graduate of CFNI, Kazushi Mitani, returned to Tokyo and married a vivacious Japanese young lady with a tremendous talent for playing the piano and singing. She had received her education in Australia, since her father worked for the government. Kazushi's father gave him land on which to build a church in the heart of Tokyo! Incredible! He then decided to produce a music tape using their own talent, both vocal and instrumental; it turned out second to none! Every visitor to their church was given a free tape (which would cost about $30 U.S.), and on the tape was printed: "Please reproduce this cassette and give it to your friends." Needless to say, when he and his wife visited me in Dallas, he told me they had to have several services each Sunday morning, and the place was packed for every meeting! What a unique way to reach their people!

So with our history of anointed praise and worship, it is not surprising that in 1995, Christ For The Nations held its first worship conference to inspire and help train true worship leaders. Our auditorium was jammed with guests, even in the overflow room. Our music leaders, Arlene Friesen, Kevin Jonas, Alex Cauthen and Anna Jeanne Price did a fabulous job!

"I will sing a new song to You, O God" (Psa. 144:9).

Chapter Six

Hitler Builds a Bible School

Can Jesus change a man's life — even if he lives on the streets of the Bronx and is a compulsive gambler and an alcoholic? Bob Humburg answers that question:

"I say yes — a thousand times yes. For that is what Jesus did for me.

"One day when I was a hopeless alcoholic and about ready to take my own life, I came into my room very early one morning and turned on the radio. The first words I heard were, 'Do you want a new life?'

"I listened to what the man had to say. He told me about Jesus Christ and the power of God to change my life. I had never had a desire to know God, but that night, September 19, 1963, I got down on my knees and invited Jesus to come into my life. I had no problem knowing I was a sinner, but from that day on, God began a work in my life and He changed me.

"Everything became new in my life. God put my family back together. He put my marriage back together. Where there had been no love in our home, the lovely Lord Jesus came in and made us new again. Our four beautiful children all came to the Lord."

In 1971, Bob and Emma's daughter, Kay, an attractive young lady from New Jersey, arrived in Dallas to attend Christ For The Nations Institute. When the year was over, she returned home.

Bob later said, "When we saw what transformation had taken place in Kay's life, it was not hard for us to move to CFNI with our entire family.

"In 1972, after I had made full restitution for the trail I had left behind me, God spoke to our hearts to go into full-time Christian service. By God's grace, our whole family came down to Christ For The Nations Institute. My wife, my two older daughters and I enrolled as students. Later, I was asked to join the staff as the director of student ministries.

"When I first came to CFNI, I thought I really had a vision from God. But as I sat under the ministry of the Spirit of God, something began to happen in my life. God gave me a vision for the whole world.

"The Bible says, 'For unto whomsoever much is given, of him shall be much required' (Lk. 12:48 KJV). God has given me much — blessing upon blessing. He has given meaning to my life, and I have a responsibility to share the Gospel of Christ with the world.

"One day, Mrs. Lindsay said to me, 'Bob, let's believe God for great things.' Those words struck fire in my heart.

"From the time we came to Christ For The Nations, we began to seek God's guidance. Then one day, a burden for Germany dropped into our hearts. But God does not speak to only one of His servants. At the same time, God began to give a vision for the work in Germany to Mrs. Lindsay, the staff and several students.

"Hundreds of years ago through Martin Luther, God brought about the Reformation which swept through

Germany and all of Europe. Multitudes forsook ritualistic traditions and put their faith in Christ. Germany became the largest Protestant country in Europe, and the Word of God took root.

"Satan failed in his attempt to keep the Bible from the German people, but he raised up men to destroy the faith in the Word of God. For many centuries, German intellectuals, philosophers and theologians attacked the Bible and exerted a disastrous influence on the Church in Europe.

"The rise of Adolph Hitler from obscurity to power, and his massacre of six million Jews, is one of the most amazing episodes of history. Because of that war, a spirit of death hung over Germany; and today, we see what the power of atheistic communism did for much of Europe.

"The German people are noted for their great industry and their remarkable rise from the ashes of defeat and destruction. What Germany produced, whether good or evil, affected the rest of the world. Being aware of the people and current prosperity of West Germany, we can realize the great potential of this nation. It is a recognized power economically, politically and industrially, but have we recognized the importance of Germany as a power for God?

"The spiritual fire that once burned fervently during the Reformation is being rekindled. Germany needs a mighty moving of the Spirit of God."

Immediately upon graduating, Bob and Emma's two beautiful daughters, Kay and Lynn (ages 23 and 21), moved to Germany with another CFNI grad and friend, Lynn. The three girls rented an inexpensive, unheated room from a German family and moved in. Kay picks up the remarkable story in a letter:

"We have been here in Germany almost 15 months now and have spent most of this time in prayer for the land. We have sought the Lord much as to what He would have us to do our first year here, and He spoke very definitely to set aside this year to concentrate on praying and interceding.

"Day by day, we have been drawing near to our Father, presenting the promises He gave us, putting Him in remembrance of His Word, and thanking Him that every promise is 'yes' in Christ Jesus. In His Name, we have said, 'Amen, let it be so in Germany to Thy glory, O God.'

"As we have prayed, a burden has deepened in our hearts. We have reminded God that He has been pouring out His Spirit in many places — but Europe and all the countries on that continent seem so bound by tradition and culture. They need the 'latter rain' of the Holy Spirit — 'for there is the sound of abundance of rain' (I Ki. 18:41). We know the Holy Spirit's burden is to get the Church of Jesus Christ cleansed and ready for the 'day of His appearing.'

"We are setting up our banners all around Germany in the victorious Name of our Lord Jesus, Who said, 'I will build my church; and the gates of hell shall not prevail against it' (Matt. 16:18 KJV).

"As the burden for Germany has deepened, a vision has become clearer and clearer in our hearts. As we have prayed, we have actually seen by faith a work that God wants to start in Germany. Christ For The Nations Institute also has begun to get a vision for a center in Germany, and many students have begun to study the language and meet together to pray."

Kay later wrote the chorus, *Ah, Lord God*. The chorus is now sung worldwide.

When the CFNI 1974 school year ended, Bob and Emma flew to Germany to look for a building for the Bible school. At the close of the summer, they had returned with photographs and descriptions of several sights. But when I saw them, I felt strongly they were not for us, for they were far too costly.

"Bob," I said, "help us here in Dallas this year, and let's concentrate with the students on praying through before you go to Germany again."

After much prayer, Bob left for Germany in June of the following year. He headed right back to the beautiful city of Braunschweig with a population of 250,000. It's only 25 minutes from the huge city of Hanover and 125 miles from Berlin. In fact, it's right on the autobahn in and out of Berlin.

The owners of a chemical factory in Braunschweig had merged their business with one in Switzerland. So they had moved, leaving vacant their building in Germany.

On the very first day Bob was in Braunschweig, he stopped to see a real estate agent. The man told Bob he was sorry, but he "didn't have a thing that would be suitable. But wait a minute ... you know, a large factory has recently been vacated. Maybe ... ." So together they drove off to see the factory.

What Bob saw was unbelievable! Here, just four blocks from the town square of Wolfenbuttel — a suburb of Braunschweig — was a hugh brick factory. It had over 45,000 square feet of floor space — two stories high.

The downstairs included a room which could be made into a beautiful auditorium, seating 700 or more. The floor was very rough, and cement would have to be poured over it. The upstairs had lovely offices, with deep mohair rugs. These could be used for dormitory rooms for about 300 men and women. There was lots of space for classrooms, a fine large dining room and two clusters of clean, beautifully-tiled shower rooms.

Bob couldn't believe what he was seeing — made to order! To replace it would cost two million dollars. We decided our business administrator, Norman Young, should fly to Germany on an economical charter flight. He had done a lot of appraising for a bank and was also a building contractor, so we felt his background would be helpful. Together, he and Bob met the owners of the factory who had flown up from Switzerland.

After two days of negotiations, Christ For The Nations bought the factory for the sum of $152,000, interest free. (This was subject to the approval of the Dallas board, which voted unanimously to buy it at once.) Only God could have done this! We paid only $2,000 down.

Several days after talking to the owner, while in prayer, Bob Humburg asked the Lord, "God, why was I led to this place the very first day?"

The Lord answered, "Robert, if you had been a blind man, I could have led you to it, with all the fasting and prayer that has come to me for that place."

During the next 12 years, the German Bible school in Braunschweig grew steadily in the same building where Hitler had stationed his crack S.S. troops years before. We remodeled the building and used it for our GlaubensZentrum (Faith Center) Bible school. But by the time this building was paid for, the school had grown so much that we needed additional housing.

So in 1983, we obtained an 80-room building recently vacated by the German Internal Revenue Service. This we also remodeled for the school's needs.

However, soon the month-end conferences at the German Bible school began to outgrow both buildings! In Europe, people often speak several languages; so spiritually hungry folk came from several nearby nations — Switzerland, Austria, Holland, Belgium and even Eastern Bloc countries — searching for more of God. The auditorium was packed with people, overflowing into the lobby and the hallway. The cafeteria couldn't handle the crowds. The dorms, too, were overflowing, and reservations couldn't be accepted.

In addition, our school's splendid 65-voice German choir sang at the Pentecostal World Conference in Switzerland, giving the school added exposure. Also, the choir rented auditoriums in four large industrial cities for weekend seminars and concerts. Each time, the auditoriums were filled, which brought more people to the conferences at GlaubensZentrum. What should we do?

Prayer was the answer. Bob Humburg urged the students and his family to stand with him in fasting and prayer. Shortly thereafter, the miracle began to unfold.

Bob learned that 45 miles from the present location (and also from the large city of Hanover), the German government was vacating a huge school it had been using to train West German border guards. The guards would combine with other trainees in another part of Germany. So that meant the beautiful and expansive buildings in Bad Gandersheim were for sale!

This news caused great excitement both at the school in Germany and back at the Dallas headquarters. Negotiations began. We learned the replacement cost for the former Nazi training camp (in excellent condition) was estimated at approximately $5 million (U.S.). Of course, we knew Christ For The Nations was not in a position to take on that amount of indebtedness. Then word came that the government would sell the building to us for about $1.3 million! We knew it had to be God.

The German bureaucracy, never known to work in haste, moved with an alacrity that surprised us. We signed the contract, and with one stroke of the pen the former Nazi school became a Bible school and a conference center ... a children's camp ... a literature depot ... a transit point for Russian Jews returning to Israel ... or whatever else the Lord had in store for us.

Yes, Hitler did it! In 1935, he set about secretly to train leaders for his intended world conquest. He chose a beautiful mineral bath resort town in the Harz Mountains to build his fortress-like camp. With thick, brick walls and a slate (stone roof) which could last through the Millennium, he erected a headquarters building in the shape of a horseshoe. The complex was sealed off with a large gate and a well-built private guardhouse at the entrance.

The town he selected was called Bad Gandersheim — "Bad" meaning bath; and Gandersheim being the surname of a Christian woman poetess who lived in the 10th century. But little did Hitler know he was building this fabulous structure for Christ For The Nations' Bible school in Germany which would train leaders to force back the powers of darkness at work in Eastern and Western Europe. It was Hitler's unintentional gift.

But the original building in Braunschweig had to be sold in order to make the payments and to make the move to Bad Gandersheim. Earnest prayer again ascended to God. Shortly thereafter, we heard that the city of Braunschweig was interested in buying the property as they were planning on opening a cultural center there across the street from the soccer field and park. After some negotiating they decided to purchase it and paid cash for it, which we immediately applied on our Bad Gandersheim school.

Then to our great surprise, we learned that as the city began to dig down several feet on the site for the cultural center, they learned the ground was contaminated and unusable due to chemicals manufactured there when Hitler was in power.

The month-end conferences have grown so large that two years ago the German school bought a beautiful hotel only a five minute walk away. It was never completely finished. So with the very exacting and precise workmanship in Germany, it is turning out to be exceedingly attractive, and is 95% completed.

Mike Chance, the son-in-law of Bob Humburg, is now the director of this amazing Bible school. He and his wife, Kay, are mightily used of God.

The Bible says in Proverbs 13:22 that the Lord would lay up the wealth of the wicked for the righteous. Praise the Lord!

Chapter Seven

Berlin Wall

Was there ever a more forboding, depressing structure in the world than the Berlin Wall that was built in Germany's capital? On our tours to Europe, we occasionally crossed over into East Berlin. The contrast was indescribable between East and West. One had to see it to believe it.

We would watch teachers, who had brought their classes to the Wall, lie to the young children that the purpose of the Wall was to keep those from the West from fleeing to the East where they could be free!

No doubt, millions of Christians were praying that the Wall would come down and the East German Christians could worship the Lord freely. Praise God, on November 9, 1989, the gates of the Berlin Wall suddenly opened up.

On our 1990 tour to Germany, after meeting two CFNI alumni pastors ministering in the city, we drove to the Berlin Wall with our tour members. With hammers and axes, we all participated in helping bring down the detested Berlin Wall. We rejoiced that God had answered multitudes of prayers, including those of Christians under communism. God had provided a way.

"Surely the wrath of man shall praise You" (Psa. 76:10).

Chapter Eight

When Bombs Are Falling

Gordon and I were standing in Jerusalem at the hotel cashier's counter, checking out, when he told me that Carole (or Shira as they call her in Israel — Shira means song or carol) had decided to stay in Israel.

"How can she? Her clothes are already on the bus leaving for Tel Aviv's airport? Besides, she has only a few clothes with her in that one suitcase," I argued.

Shira had mentioned before we left Dallas that she might stay in Israel. And Gordon had cautioned me not to say one word to her about it. "If it's of God, she'll stay. If not, she won't," was his admonition.

But that early morning, I was a long way from being ready to leave Shira in Jerusalem, especially since Israel had just finished the 1967 Six Day War. How could I leave my only daughter in Israel?

The three of us climbed into the bus; little was said on the one-hour trip to Tel Aviv. Upon arriving, Gordon pulled out Shira's suitcase and set it aside. We said our goodbyes, kissed and I hurried away, as I didn't want Shira to see me crying.

But I felt like Hannah when she left her only son, little Samuel, with Eli the prophet — forever! The difference between Hannah and me was that she could praise and worship the Lord, while all I could do was weep. One thing we two did have in common: I, too, felt my child was the Lord's forever.

The years went by, with Shira determined to minister to the people of Israel. Eventually, she met a man named Ari Sorko-Ram in Los Angeles. His mother was Jewish, so he had an interest in Israel. And after living in Israel for six months, Ari came with Shira to Dallas, where they were married five days later. The two returned to Israel. Two children were soon born to them: a son, Ayal, and a daughter, Shani. They started a messianic Jewish congregation, have been involved in producing films, have ministered on the streets of Tel Aviv through music and drama, and most recently, held an Israeli youth camp and three adult seminars.

When Operation Desert Storm began, I increased my prayer time. Exactly 39 Scuds fell in Israel from Iraq, and America had warned Israel not to retaliate — the first time Israel could not defend herself.

Each time it was announced a Scud had just fallen in Israel, I could picture my daughter and her family in Tel Aviv as they ran for their bomb shelter, wearing gas masks. Sometimes in the middle of our phone conversations, the sirens would start blowing, and they'd have to hang up and run to the shelter. I wanted to call every time I heard a Scud had fallen, but decided to restrain myself.

I recall my granddaughter, Shani, 12 years old at the time, saying to me, "Be sure you pray for my little dog, too. She wears a gas mask, and I don't want her to die either." We all prayed here, and praise God, He spared their lives!

I was able to be in Israel to attend the bar and bat mitzvah of my grandchildren. Present for the sacred occasion were their school friends, neighbors, believers and nonbelievers, and of course, members of their congregation. Thank God, my grandchildren know the Word well!

Though God did give Israel a stern warning: Thirty-nine Scuds fell, not a single Israeli died from that attack. In the Bible when a sinner was scourged for his evil, he received forty stripes save one — 39 total, lest he perish from the lashes. God's mercy again had been extended to Israel.

But the revival in Israel — a nationwide turning to the Messiah — has not come. Recently, bombs of another sort have begun falling!

According to Zechariah 13:8, eventually there will be another holocaust! Our own America will be involved in that and brought to the valley of Jehoshaphat for judgment (Joel 3:2,3; Dan. 5:28). We were the ones who urged Israel into signing the so-called "Peace Process" at the White House on September 13, 1993, to divide that nation.

At CFNI in Dallas, we teach our students to pray daily for Israel. Atop our headquarters, we fly two flags — America's and Israel's.

Chapter Nine

In Israel for Rabin's Funeral

Our 30th Israel tour group landed in Frankfurt, Germany, on November 4, 1995. That night, we learned that Prime Minister Yitzhak Rabin had just been assassinated in Tel Aviv. He had spoken there at a peace rally attended by 100,000 of both his many supporters and Arabs (half of the large crowd it was said). Leaving the rally, Rabin was shot twice as he was going to his car in a small, dark parking lot. The assailant was a 27-year-old Jewish law student.

On Sunday, November 5, at 1 p.m. when our tour group left Germany for Israel, the airbus was loaded to the hilt with newsmen and their cameras. They were in a hurry to get to Israel for Rabin's funeral the next day.

After checking in at the hotel with our group that night, I decided to go to Jerusalem the next day for the funeral. The next morning, Randy Bozarth, a capable CFNI faculty member and overseer of our foreign Bible schools, left with our group for the Galilee as scheduled. Meanwhile, I took a cab to our Jerusalem Center where I was met by Charles and Elizabeth Kopp, with whom we have worked for 20 years.

At 12:30 p.m., Charles, Elizabeth and I started by car toward the Mt. Hertzl Cemetery where Rabin's funeral was to take place. After we drove a short distance, police ordered us to stop and pointed to a spot where Charles was to park his car. So the three of us took off on foot. For over two miles we "climbed" the mountainous sidewalks of Jerusalem. The closer we came to Mt. Hertzl, the larger the crowds — hundreds of thousands, mostly teen-agers and soldiers, young men and women, with a scattering of older folk.

At the entrance to the cemetery, we were all stopped by guards, as only 5,000 were being allowed in to attend the actual funeral held in a makeshift amphitheater near Theodore Hertzl's grave. Among those allowed to attend were heads of state and senior officials from about 85 countries, including six from Arab nations. An estimated one million had filed by Rabin's casket as it lay in state on Sunday at the Knesset.

Not since the assassination of President John Kennedy have so many heads of state gathered in a nation for a memorial service. At Israel's Ben Gurion airport, 90 planes carrying the most important people had arrived on Monday. On the ground were 20 Air Force helicopters in waiting, along with 80 buses and numerous embassy cars and limousines.

Four planes had brought the U.S. delegation to Israel: President and Mrs. Clinton, former presidents George Bush and Jimmy Carter, Senate Majority Leader Robert Dole, House Speaker Newt Gingrich, former Secretary of State George Schultz, Secretary of State Warren Christopher, and many senators and House members.

At 2 p.m., a citywide blowing of car horns and a siren

pierced the air announcing the official start of the funeral service. At that sound, everyone "froze" to attention. The youth all around us stood for the two minutes without moving a muscle.

The Kopps and I joined a large group of young people sitting on the pavement listening to the eulogies on the radio. Among the speakers were Jordan's King Hussein, Egyptian President Hosni Mubarek, Russian Prime Minister Viktor Chernomyrden, U.N. Secretary-General Boutros Boutros-Ghali, Spanish Prime Minister Felipe Gonzalez, U.S. President William Clinton, Acting Prime Minister Shimon Peres, two longtime Rabin aides, and Rabin's granddaughter.

Peres had, the day before, told the Knesset, "Fear for the future fills my heart. Boundless and unending fear." This is the profile of a man who is at best, an agnostic and at worst, an atheist — a man without faith in God!

During the more than two hours of the funeral service, I watched the young people with whom we were listening. They sat stone-faced in total silence, smoking one cigarette after another, burning their memorial candles. Some wiped away tears, while others buried their faces in their hands. It is the youth of Israel who have the most to gain if peace comes, and the most to lose if Israel goes to war.

Once the funeral service was over, eight men — six major-generals and two senior police officers carried the flag-draped coffin on their shoulders to the grave. One by one, the long sleek limousines with darkened windows, carrying official heads of government, raced down Mt. Hertzl with police escorts to leave the country. Among them were Jordan's King Hussein with American-born Queen No'or, his prime minister, and a large entourage including 39 bodyguards. Israel had 10,000 security on hand.

Not present at the funeral was PLO Chairman Yasser Arafat. Israel had advised him not to come for security reasons. (He did make a historic first trip to Israel to visit Rabin's widow, Leah, but it was not announced that he had done so until he was safely back in Arab territory. Leah welcomed Arafat, but she had difficulty shaking hands with the opposition leader Benjamin Netanyahu, whom she blamed for the assassination.)

Nor did Syria's president, Hafez Assad, attend the funeral. He called for Israel's total withdrawal from "all occupied Arab lands including the Golan Heights." The government newspaper, *Tishrin*, urged Israel, "to abandon the policy of wasting time ... if it is really willing to achieve peace." It was reported that people in some Arab nations, as well as some in Israel, danced in the streets when they heard of Rabin's death.

When our tour returned from Galilee, we, along with thousands of others, visited the grave of Rabin in a downpour of rain. The 10' x 10' plot was stacked with several feet of flowers. While flags everywhere were flying at half-mast, Israel's president, Ezer Weizman, announced he would not set up a new government until the week of mourning was over.

Israel will hold its national election in 1996. In the meantime, Prime Minister Shimon Peres carries on in the footsteps of Rabin. For you may recall it was Peres who signed the official "Peace Process" agreement in the White House on September 13, 1993 — at President Clinton's urging. God tells what will happen to those who divide up His land in Joel 3:1,2.

Only a few days before his death, when Rabin asked for a vote of confidence for his government, the Knesset voted 61-59 for him. A tie would have given him no confidence. He won by one vote; one less would have been a tie. And since there are half a dozen Arabs in the Knesset, that meant, since they naturally favored Rabin's "Peace Process," it was the Arabs' votes that won for him and not the Jewish.

His unpopularity was, of course, due to the fact he gave Jericho and Bethlehem to Arafat and the PLO, and was in the process of giving them the West Bank. The Golan Heights and even Jerusalem were up for future negotiations. In death, Rabin suddenly became a hero, virtually a god. For many Jews are atheists or agnostics and have no other god — little or no hope.

True, Israel was in a state of mourning. The reason? I read it in their papers and heard from an Israeli: "A Jew killed a Jew." In 2,000 years, no Jewish prime minister had been assassinated by a Jew! But the families of the nearly 800 Israelis who have been killed by terrorists since the "Peace Process" began — far more than in any similar time before "peace" began — stand unconvinced.

And, too, the Arabs have fought six wars with Israel since she declared herself a nation in 1948, and they have lost every one! Now the Arabs are using the "Peace

Process" — demanding one piece of Israel's land at a time. Shortly, Israel will not be able to defend herself as at her mid-center she will be only 12 miles wide.

Yigal Amir, who killed Prime Minister Rabin, said he had also planned to kill Foreign Minister Shimon Peres. Amir said that the two leaders were guilty of shaking the hand of murderers who are freeing terrorists from prison so they can murder Jews within days. He asked, "Haven't the Israeli people noticed that a Palestinian state is being established here? As soon as a person turns his people and his land over to the enemy, he must be killed according to our *Halacha*." Israel has freed from prison thousands of terrorists who are now being armed as police or PLO militia.

But we must never forget, God is in control! "For exaltation (promotion) *comes* neither from the east nor the west nor from the south. But God is the Judge: He puts down one, and exalts another" (Psa. 75:6,7). "Pray for the peace of Jerusalem: they shall prosper that love thee" (Psa. 122:6 KJV).

(Update: In May 1996, Israeli voters rejected Shimon Peres and elected conservative Benjamin Netanyahu as prime minister — shocking the world! Netanyahu went to the Western Wall to pray just before and following his victory. He pledges peace with security; that Jerusalem, the Golan Heights and Hebron are not negotiable; and that Israeli settlements will continue to be built in the West Bank. His margin of election victory was 11.5%. This landslide came from Jewish voters and some Arabs who felt safer living under Israeli rule than under the Palestinians. Netanyahu will need constant prayer.)

Chapter Ten

The Desert Blossoms

"So Moses brought Israel from the Red Sea; then they went out into the Wilderness of Shur. And they went three days in the wilderness and found no water. Now when they came to Marah, they could not drink the waters of Marah, for they were bitter. Therefore the name of it was called Marah" (Ex. 15:22,23).

A barren, desolate wilderness: That's what the Sinai and the Negev deserts are. Where not a blade of grass grows! Worthless!

The children of Israel, coming from Egypt, came through this area located in the southern end of what is now Israel. Two million strong, along with their cattle, they tromped for three days through this wilderness and stopped at a roadside village, a "truck-stop" called Marah. They needed water badly. When they tasted what they found, it was bitter! They cried to Moses, who in turn called on the Lord for help. God showed Moses a tree, told him to throw it into the water, and the waters were made sweet!

Professor Arie Isser, an Israeli scientist at the Ben-Gurion University of the Negev, determined that waters of Marah seemed strikingly similar to the waters that flow from the springs of the Dead Sea — hundreds of miles away. When he tested water samples from both locations, he found they were identical chemically.

After further research, he discovered a literal vast ocean of water trapped underground. Conventional wisdom said that since the water was laced with epsom salts and gypsum, it could never be used for agriculture. Wrong!

Epsom salts are a laxative. Sometimes life's situations leave us feeling wrung out. No doubt, God allows these times to flush out carnal things from our lives.

And what about the gypsum? It is a white powdered mineral that when mixed with water becomes a hard plaster of paris. This is used for plasterboard in buildings or for casts to set broken arms, legs, etc. These casts slow down the mobility of the person. Does God sometimes slow us down for a period of healing and meditation so He can speak to us when we're alone?

By using the newly discovered water to irrigate the desert, today crops like wheat, tomatoes and even watermelons and cucumbers flourish in this so-called "worthless" desert!

Doesn't God say in Isaiah 35:1,2: "And the desert shall rejoice and blossom as the rose; it shall blossom abundantly and rejoice, even with joy and singing"?

Are there desert areas in your life — unused talents, untapped potential that God wants to use? Let God turn bitter experiences in your life to fruitful growth periods.

Chapter Eleven

Songs in the Night

One morning about 3 a.m., I woke up singing, *At the Foot of the Cross*. I didn't remember when I had ever heard it. But it kept coming back again and again as I lay in bed humming it. So after a time, I turned on the light and wrote down the words.

At the foot of the cross I found Jesus.
At the foot of the cross I found healing.
At the foot of the cross I found peace and joy within,
Broke the bonds of binding sins,
Saw God's plan for fallen man.
Now I live for Him alone,
For my sins He did atone,
When I knelt at the foot of the cross.

Another song the Lord gave me which expresses my commitment to God is *Holding Nothing*.

Holding nothing; holding nothing;
All I am I give to You to choose to use.
Holding nothing; holding nothing.
All I am and all I have belongs to You.
All I am and all I have belongs to You.

Lacking nothing; lacking nothing.
All my needs You have supplied

Each day by day.
Lacking nothing; lacking nothing.
You have proved Your Word is true along life's way.
You have proved Your Word is true along life's way.

To my surprise, our students sang it on our annual chorus tape. It's always exciting when I visit in foreign lands and congregations sing these songs to me in their own language.

"In the night His song shall be with me — a prayer to the God of my life" (Psa. 42:8).

Chapter Twelve

The First Proclaimed Atheist Nation

For many years, millions of Christians have prayed daily for Albania, the first openly-declared atheist nation. In the summer of 1995, it was my privilege to lead a tour group to Albania, the nation that had been under the iron grip of atheism for 50 years.

Dictator Enver Hoxja ruled the land for 44 years. In 1967, he proclaimed Albania to be the first atheistic country. *Church Around the World* reported that in 1991 there were only 16 known believers left in that country. All the churches had been turned into markets and museums, and Sunday became a day when people worked free for the state.

Hoxja outlawed religion and enforced the ban with a vengeance. He meant for Albania to be a showpiece for communism — proof that the godless state would work. Children were taught to worship and sing to Hoxja; he was their god. He worked closely with Stalin. He died of a heart attack in 1985. Then in November 1990, a student revolution took place, opening that poor nation of three million to the outside world.

Some 70% of the Albanians are Muslims, 20% are

Catholic and 10% are Orthodox (which now includes about 12,000 Christians). Muslims are pouring millions of dollars into the land — building mosques, hospitals and banks open only to Muslims.

However, in the same building once used for the Communist Party congresses, the *Jesus* film was shown to an overflow crowd of 2,200 political leaders, says Don Mansfield, director of Campus Crusade. Last year, the *Jesus* film was shown in 253 Albanian villages, with an average of 15% of the viewers making decisions for Christ.

We were told there are 70-80 churches, including some house-groups of four, five or six people. One church is said to have 300. Ulf Ekman, the pastor of a huge faith-church in Sweden, has provided a number of short-term Bible schools in some of the villages and in Tirana, the capital with 200,000 people. Three young Albanian women who attended one of the schools believed the faith teaching and began to pray for the sick. In Durres, the National Hospital was emptied and remained empty for an entire month after these three women had been there to pray, reports Ekman.

While we were in Albania, through the generosity of a couple who are friends of Christ For The Nations and have a burden for that country, we were able to deliver 30,000 New Testaments printed on the former communist presses my son Gilbert is using in Belarus.

We were surprised to find an Albanian couple laboring among the Muslims. They have, unbeknownst to us, translated, printed and distributed many thousands of Gordon Lindsay's books. They reported to us that the

Muslims love these books because they can understand them. Only heaven will reveal what God has been able to accomplish through the generosity of faithful donors who have stood with us through the years.

The former private physician to dictator Hoxja, Sali Berisha, is now president. Not much has changed economically. Some 60% of the people are unemployed. They say, "No bread, no water, no electricity." (Our tour group experienced this while trying to take showers. Sometimes we were fortunate to have even cold or cool water.)

It was my delight — and that of Randy Bozarth — to minister in Tirana to the students of a Bible school which Rev. Billy Joe Daugherty of Tulsa has started. How receptive and joyful the students were as our tour members prayed over each one.

But as we returned home, the picture that remained in my mind was that of the military bunkers Hoxja built in Albania — 700,000 of them! We saw them everywhere from the moment we stepped from the plane — along every road, on every farm, every hill, along the coast! Incredible! This paranoid dictator feared the United States (or Greece or China — or anybody) was going to invade Albania! We were told that had he used the concrete and heavy steel for something useful, he would have had enough material to build 700,000 homes for his impoverished people. But fear gripped his heart.

The Bible says, "There is no peace ... for the wicked" (Isa. 48:22). Hoxja was one of history's glaring examples of this truth. ... Today several Albanian students are attending CFNI in Dallas. No nation can shut out God!

"Thus says the LORD of hosts: 'Consider your ways! ... And he who earns wages, earns wages to *put* into a bag with holes'" (Hag. 1:5,6).

Chapter Thirteen

Synagogue Reaches Thousands for Jesus

Read this amazing story:

These days we see and hear so much about the war in the former Yugoslavia, which has broken up into several ethnic nations — Croatia being one of them. In Osijek, there was an old, beautiful Jewish synagogue, no longer in use as the Jewish population had pretty much disappeared. Because this building had so deteriorated, the city planned to destroy it. Several believers in the city asked the government for possession of it in exchange for restoring it. Their request was granted.

So in 1980, Christ For The Nations gave $17,100 toward this restoration. A few years later, I spoke in several churches in what was then Yugoslavia and was scheduled for a convention in Osijek. When we drove up to the conference sight, to my great surprise and joy, I recognized the synagogue we had helped restore. Dr. Peter Kuzmic was the pastor there and had also started a Bible school in the synagogue.

One night, I preached on the baptism in the Holy Spirit; many came forward and were filled. The next morning as I spoke again, a man stood up weeping and waving his "arms."

I asked the pastor, "What is he saying?"

He replied, "He received the Holy Spirit last night and was awake all through the night, laughing and crying for joy. For it is the first time since he lost both of his hands in the war that he has ever felt he had a reason to live." It was then that instead of hands I noticed that he had two clumsy hooks fastened to his arms!

Recently, I wondered, with all the fighting in the area, how is that church and school doing? So we wrote asking. Back came this reply: "Attacks on our town started in September 1991, with shelling from three sides. In the next six months, 150,000 shells fell, which destroyed one-third of our industry and many apartments in our town of 140,000. When a neighboring town, Vukovar, fell, everyone expected Osijek to be next. But God was merciful and heard our prayers; not even one shell fell on our complex. God has protected this whole campus because here we train good missionaries for the future.

"Osijek is still surrounded on three sides, for the front is about three miles from our school, and 500,000 refugees have moved into our city. We are helping to feed and clothe many of these refugees. And the good news is that we now have 90 Bible students from 27 countries of Eastern Europe and Africa.

"Until now, we are the biggest seminary for master's degree studies in Eastern Europe. We have translated and are using some of Gordon Lindsay's books. Your

Living Praise singers and other graduates have helped us here, for which we thank you." A.B., Chief Executive Officer.

God is our protector in war times!

"A thousand may fall at your side, and ten thousand at your right hand; but it shall not come near you. Only with your eyes shall you look, and see the reward of the wicked" (Psa. 91:7,8).

Chapter Fourteen

God Chooses a Prison

The well-known evangelist Benny Hinn came to speak at CFNI. A young man from Bulgaria, George Michailov, was on campus to hear him. After the service, I introduced them to each other, and the evangelist invited George to be with him in several services.

George had been trained in college as an engineer. He had a good job, was married and had one child. His sister was married to a Christian minister, Pastor Stefanov, who was constantly harassed, imprisoned and beaten for allowing children to attend the meetings — along with his own two sons.

After the final arrest, the pastor was taken to the Troyan police station where his head was repeatedly bashed against the wall. His beatings were so severe that though he was allowed to return home, he died soon thereafter.

For years, the pastor's sister had allowed believers to meet secretly in her large concealed basement. Many attended, quietly coming and going. In one of the services, an elderly man arose and prophesied that the very same prison in which Pastor Stefanov was beaten to the point of death, would become a house of God — a church.

When George heard of his brother-in-law's death,

he was greatly moved upon by the Lord: Would he resign his good-paying (for Bulgaria) position and carry on the spread of the Gospel in Pastor Stefanov's place? After much soul-searching, he and his wife gave God the answer: "Yes." George resigned his position and began preaching as best he could.

Soon after, George wrote me asking if the eldest of Stefanov's sons could attend CFNI on a scholarship. We agreed. Soon the other son arrived, too. When they completed their studies, they returned to Bulgaria to become pastors.

Then George wrote asking for help to buy property for a church and Bible school, instead of renting and being evicted at the whim of the owner. CFN conducted a tour to Bulgaria, and we were able to help him purchase property for that purpose.

While in Lovech, Bulgaria, I was invited to speak on a Sunday morning in Troyan. Then I learned that the original police station had been moved to another area of the city. An assembly, the outgrowth of the underground Church which regularly met in Stefanov's sister's basement, had acquired the use of the police station for services.

Can you imagine my great joy to be a witness to the fulfillment of that prophecy and to be allowed to speak to such a consecrated congregation in such a solemn facility? God be praised!

"O LORD God, to whom vengeance belongs — O God, to whom vengeance belongs, shine forth! Rise up, O Judge of the earth; Render punishment to the proud" (Psa. 94:1,2).

Chapter Fifteen

We Found God's Plan in a Dark Nation

John Dolinschi, a dedicated young preacher, and his brother-in-law had escaped on foot from Romania. Once in the United States, John found a job in Arizona and began saving his money. When he later enrolled at CFNI, he was able to pay for two full years.

Occasionally, he would load his suitcases with Bibles, clothes and food and return to his homeland, preaching secretly to underground groups with the knowledge of an official with whom he had attended high school.

Suddenly, it seemed in Romania opposition arose against the ruthless Communist dictator, Nicolai Ceausescu. A few days later, he was assassinated! There was now freedom to preach the Gospel openly!

Now John felt God had given him a vision to train men and women for the ministry in Romania. He prayerfully and carefully selected seven young men to attend CFNI. He was able to buy inexpensive airline tickets for each of them. In Dallas, we provided the scholarships for their schooling. On June 12, 1990, seven clean-cut, serious, young men arrived in Dallas from Romania. Most were married and had left their families behind. They came to train for the ministry. At year's end, they returned to their homes and families in Timisoara and Suceava.

Now that staff members were trained and ready, property and buildings were necessary. So in two cities, Timisoara and Suceava, we bought a large house and the Bible schools began.

On June 12, 1994, exactly four years to the day from when the seven young Romanians came to Dallas to study, it was my great privilege to dedicate the beautiful new 500-seat Bible school auditorium in Timisoara which Christ For The Nations had helped build.

On the platform with me were my dear friends of many years, Stanley and Helen Walters from Washington state. Again and again, they had given generously to make possible overseas projects. It was they who had paid outright the full price for the very strategic land on which both the Timisoara and Suceava schools stand. The Timisoara school now has over 200 students, and the one in Suceava, with a building under construction, has 50.

Christ For The Nations is not the only ministry that moved with haste to respond when Romania's door opened to the Gospel. Tent meetings held by evangelists Walter and Edith Kronberg, another precious couple and friends of CFN for many years, caused churches to spring up all over Romania. Thousands were saved and healed under the Kronbergs' big tent. God provides what is needed. We are thankful for all those who willingly sacrifice to take God's message of love to the nations.

"Blessed are you who sow beside all waters" (Isa. 32:20).

Chapter Sixteen

Vail

It was Sunday, August 9, the last day of summer school and the final day of our Annual Retreat. It had been a hectic school year with trips to Jamaica, Israel, Honduras, Nicaragua, Hawaii, and several conventions, seminars, interviews, summer school, plus the daily workload of the office with articles, endorsements, correspondence, etc. The heat that day seemed to make me extra weary, and I was really looking forward to my annual week's vacation with my two sons and their families at Vail, Colorado, where Gilbert at that time owned a condo.

As soon as the Sunday afternoon service was over, I headed for the airport to catch a plane to Denver. Upon arrival there, I hurried to the shuttle bus to take me to Vail — a trip of nearly three hours. I was anticipating a nice, cool quiet drive through the mountains, as it was now getting dark.

When I found my bus, a scrawny young man in cutoffs smoking a cigarette was standing beside it. Immediately, I had some misgivings. But in a few moments all the Vail passengers climbed into the bus; I picked a seat behind the driver.

As soon as we were on our way, the driver turned on

a tape of loud blaring rock music. Was this the time of relaxation to which I had so looked forward? Hardly! What to do?

I began to pray. The passengers were all getting acquainted. All were from middle- or upper-class families. People like myself, don't usually spend vacations in Vail. The lady beside me said she was going there to check on her two fur stores.

After about an hour, I suddenly remembered a tape that Mike Adkins, my favorite singer, had given me a couple of nights previously when he held a concert at CFNI. I had the tape in my purse!

I pulled it out and handed it to the driver saying, "Here's a tape I believe you'll like. It's by a friend who has several gold albums to his credit." He handed it to the passenger beside him, who had earlier told us he was just returning from Australia, where he had worked on his doctorate. This gentleman pulled off the cellophane and handed it back to the driver who began to play it.

After a few minutes, I heard the driver say, "This fellow sounds like he's into religion." The tape rolled on. After some time, Mike began to sing his famous *Adoration*, in tongues! Things got awfully quiet. By now, everyone in the bus had stopped talking while I was quietly praying "up a storm" that God would touch the hearts of these people who seemed so financially secure that they probably felt they didn't need God!

When the tape finished, the driver suddenly called out, "Anybody ready for a drink?" as he pulled off the highway. When he stopped the bus, everyone jumped off and headed for the store. Most, it seemed, settled for a can of beer. I chose a bottle of red strawberry soda.

We all gathered outside in a circle by the side of the bus and enjoyed the cool night in the 10,000-feet-high mountains. Unexpectedly, a fast-moving car with "Sheriff" painted on the side of it, came to a quick stop beside our group. Getting out of the car, a tall man in uniform walked right over to where we were standing.

Looking at me, he asked abruptly, "Are you Freda Lindsay?" I didn't know whether I should answer him or not! What had I done? Was there an emergency?

Slowly, I replied, "Yes."

Then he responded warmly, "I thought that was you. I've attended several of your seminars in Dallas, and I felt sure when I looked this way it was you. I've enjoyed them so much."

At that moment, I looked down at the red bottle of strawberry soda and thought, "What if I had in my hand a can of beer, thinking, 'I'm away from home. Nobody would find it out up here?'" I could have ruined my testimony in a split second. I was thankful that I hadn't even been tempted to have a beer to drink.

By now, several of the passengers were curious. "Driving as fast as you were in the darkness at 11 p.m. in these mountains, how could you ever have recognized her?"

He replied, "I don't know. When I looked over, I recognized her the moment I saw her." We talked a bit, then he drove away.

As soon as we returned to our bus, the questions came thick and fast. "Who are you? What do you do?" etc.

My answer, "I'm just a nobody." But I was ready. For

the next hour, I gave them my testimony of how the Lord had saved me, healed me of tuberculosis in both lungs when I was 24 years old, and all about Christ For The Nations, etc. Several members of the group wanted my address, which I readily supplied for them.

It was midnight when we arrived at the condo. Both of my sons, Gilbert and Dennis, were up waiting for me. As I left the bus, the passengers hollered, "Good night, Freda. Great knowing you!"

I suppose my sons are still wondering, "What made Mom so popular all of a sudden?" God will make a way to witness if we wait for His direction.

"The Lord is ... not willing that any should perish but that all should come to repentance" (II Pet. 3:9).

Chapter Seventeen

We Need New Furniture

Ginger Lindsay, my son Dennis' wife, was to be in charge of the new women's conference we were initiating in 1990. She is so exacting about everything she does that Dennis said concerning her, "She takes all year to plan and prepare for this three-day women's conference!"

After looking over the housing facilities on campus, Ginger decided the ladies coming for that conference should be housed on the upper floors of Gordon Lindsay Tower, our men's dormitory which was originally a Sheraton hotel!

Only one minor problem: She felt the furniture in the rooms was not suitable for the occasion. So she came to me saying, "We need new furniture for those rooms."

Now we had another problem: There was no money for new furniture. The students' tuition at CFNI has to be subsidized each year by one-fourth to one-third. The school does not pay for itself. We purposely set the fees at reasonable rates so students with families can afford to come, too. So I told Ginger that if she wanted furniture badly enough, she needed to start praying for it — and start looking for a hotel or motel going out of business.

Two weeks later, she came to me all excited. She had noticed that a nice new motel near the airport had apparently closed. It had a big "Furniture For Sale" sign on it.

Together with our maintenance supervisor, we jumped in the car and sped to the motel. Several trucks and cars were already there. The beautiful solid wood furniture was like 99¾% new. Some of it had never been used even once.

I immediately contacted the manager and offered to buy 26-rooms worth of furniture for $10,000. We would give him a tax deduction receipt for the balance of its worth.

He said he had no authority to do anything except sell for cash. When I questioned him on who had that authority, he answered, "My boss in Chicago."

"Call him," I urged.

I made the boss the same offer, as Ginger and I prayed. In a minute, his answer was, "Yes, it's a deal."

Our truck came to pick up the merchandise within the hour. Ginger's prayers had been answered. We had chests of drawers, game tables, chairs, lamps, end tables, mattresses, table lamps, even pictures for the walls. God promised to supply all our needs (Phil. 4:19).

Chapter Eighteen

Above and Beyond

It was January 25, 1985, the second day of our Winter Retreat. Marilyn Hickey was the night speaker. Our friendship with Marilyn goes back to the late '40s; I admire her greatly. Her teaching is always stimulating to me.

On this particular Friday night, I had emceed the service and when finished, I left the platform to sit in the audience near the rear of the packed auditorium.

That night as she preached, Marilyn told a story. She related how several years earlier she "knew" God was going to give her a fur coat. She told her husband, Wally, "It's going to be full-length, brown, fox, size 6." He replied with a laugh, "I'm not buying you a fur coat!"

She responded, "God will supply it!"

Time passed. When she'd be in revivals, she'd call home. Wally would tease her with, "Has God sent your fur coat yet?"

"No, but He will," was her answer, to which Wally would laugh heartily.

One day, while Wally was in a jewelry store to have a watch repaired, in walked another customer. In her conversation with the proprietor, the woman said, "My husband bought me a nice fur coat not long before he died. I really didn't need it as I already have a couple. Do you know of anyone who would want a brown, full-length, size 6, fox fur coat?"

Wally, though surprised, responded with, "I know a lady that will fit that coat exactly."

"Come get it," said the customer, and she gave him her address.

Wally picked up the coat without delay, then phoned Marilyn who was in another city on a speaking tour. Excitedly, he told Marilyn, "Guess what! You won't believe this!"

Before he could finish, she replied, "Oh yes, I will. You've got a fur coat for me: fox, brown, full-length, size 6!"

And so it was. Wally didn't buy it. God had sent it!

But now I'm sitting there in the auditorium having a "pity party." "God, you haven't given me a fur coat, and I've served you many years. And besides, next week I'm to go to Washington D.C. for a convention where they've been having snow and sleet, with more predicted."

Soon after, Marilyn finished her teaching and I left the auditorium, not through the door from the lobby, as usual, but using the one in the Fellowship Hall. As I passed the office, the secretary called, "Oh, Mrs. Lindsay, I'm glad I caught you. Can you stop in for a moment? A lady came in earlier to say she has a coat for you. Can you wait for her?" I decided to wait.

Immediately, I saw a blue fabric coat on the chair and concluded that must be the one. Blue had always been my favorite color, so it pleased me. "Why not try it on?" I thought, but decided it was more appropriate to wait until this "anonymous" person came to hand it to me.

Before long, a doctor's friendly wife from out of the city entered the office. She and her husband had attended our seminars a number of times. After we greeted one another, she added, "The Lord told me today to buy you a coat."

I smiled and thought, "I hope she obeyed!" as I waited for her to hand me the blue cloth coat. Instead, she turned to leave, saying, "Wait, and I'll go to the car and get it."

Shortly, she returned with a Neiman Marcus garment bag! That's Dallas' number one store where first ladies often buy dresses for inaugurations and other very glitzy occasions!

She started with, "I know you are very conservative, so I hope you'll like this one. It is reversible with poplin on one side; sheared muskrat on the other, trimmed all the way down with wide fox fur." As she unzipped the garment bag, out came this beautiful beige coat!

"Oh, they left the price tag on it!" she exclaimed. As she and I "struggled" to take the tag off with the help of the secretary at the desk who couldn't find a pair of scissors, I "accidentally on purpose" noticed the cost — $6,000! I could scarcely believe that this little girl born in a sod house in Canada of parents born in Russia, so poor our clothes often came from the Salvation Army store, would one day wear such a fabulous coat!

Six days later, I left Dallas in sleet and arrived in

snowy Washington D.C. for the convention. Never did I enjoy wearing anything more than my nice, warm fur coat. And for the past 10 years, it has accompanied me many times in freezing weather. Yes, God does do "exceedingly abundantly above all that we ask or think, according to the power that works in us, to Him be glory" (Eph. 3:20, 21).

Later, when I related this "coat miracle" to Marilyn, I guess she figured I "owed" her a "return favor." She invited me to speak at her Washington D.C. Women's Conference on "Women in Dominion" with 4,000 present and then to her convention in Los Angeles, where I helped her raise her budget and speak on "Winning Women."

Chapter Nineteen

Extinguished the Raging Fire

It was Commencement Sunday, May 8, 1988 at CFNI. Reinhard Bonnke was our speaker. Some 308 were graduating — always an exciting time.

The next day, some students began leaving either on outreaches or for home, while others stayed on for the summer session. The deans were putting the remaining students into one area of the dormitories to make room for seminar guests, to allow for painting and general maintenance, as well as to cut the cost of the utilities.

Dennis and I had speaking commitments in South Texas and Mexico. After winding down with several immediate responsibilities, we flew to Nuevo Laredo, Mexico, then visited four unbelievably pitiful squatters' camps to distribute food and clothing. At 2 a.m. on the night of the second day we received a phone call that our girls' dorm in Dallas, Mary Martha, had been devastated by fire.

Our first concern was for our dean of women, Sally Horton, who lived in the dorm and for the girls who had stayed for the summer school that we had moved to one end of that very dorm. Were they all OK? The gratifying answer was, "Yes," though a few, including Sally, had lost their possessions. Sally had taken an outreach to Great Britain. We prayed earnestly for them.

Five days later, after finishing our speaking engagements, Dennis and I flew back to Dallas. Of course, we first wanted to see the girls from Mary Martha. Next, we wanted to see the extent of the fire. About two-thirds of the building was nearly destroyed! What the flames didn't ruin, the smoke did.

When Sally returned from her outreach, having been told about the fire, she was pleasantly surprised; she had expected the worst. Her important papers, her best family photos and her good jewelry were all salvaged. The roof had fallen in on her antique four-poster bed and her dining room set, but neither was damaged.

Though some heavy shelves had fallen on her china and crystal, the dishes were not cracked or broken — not even chipped. The firemen later told Sally that had she been in the apartment when the fire broke out, she would not have gotten out alive.

Fortunately, we had insurance for the fire. Several estimates had to be collected. We settled for the amount agreed upon and decided to use our own maintenance crew to do some of the work.

The amazing thing was that Mary Martha was the oldest dormitory on our campus and badly needed some upgrading. When the crew finished with the renovation just in time for the fall semester, the apartments looked brand new. A new roof, cabinets, walls, floors, carpeting — everything! All paid for with the insurance money!

God had again miraculously "provided provision" in the face of adversity!

"Who through faith ... obtained promises ... quenched the violence of fire" (Heb. 11:33,34).

Chapter Twenty

Lost and Found

It was time for our annual seminar in Montego Bay, Jamaica. This was an occasion to which many have looked forward all year long. Guests were arriving from all over the United States, Canada and some of the islands.

Our 13-acre campus in Jamaica is actually one of the world's beauty spots. It overlooks the bay, is covered with flowers, has trees of many kinds including stately palms.

Denise, my secretary, arrived at Montego Bay with other guests for our seminar. Vans and trucks were waiting at the airport for our visitors and their luggage. When the guests arrived at our Caribbean campus just seven miles from the airport and the suitcases were distributed, Denise's bag was missing. She was certain she had seen her baggage by the side of the campus truck as the luggage was being loaded at the airport. A careful search on the campus produced no clue. Prayer was made since the suitcase contained Denise's good clothes, plus over $1,000 worth of supplies for the little shop we have on the campus.

Four days went by; no sign of the suitcase. Then some members of the campus staff went to the airport to pick up more guests; lo and behold, there in plain sight on the sidewalk, unattended, stood Denise's bag — with everything intact!

January is Jamaica's busiest time of the year. Thousands of tourists had come and gone in those four days, but not one had touched that bag, which apparently was inadvertently left sitting there when the other luggage was being loaded onto the campus truck. "Providential protection," for sure!

But a greater miracle took place when God "found" Jamaica-born Peter Burnett. Though reared by a godly mother, he never even knew his father. He was age 15 when one of our CFNI summer outreaches ministered in Jamaica. The team decided to go swimming in the ocean on their day off, and Peter joined them. Shortly after, the undertow pulled him out to sea. One CFNI student who tried to rescue him nearly drowned in the effort. A second student was successful in bringing back Peter's lifeless body to the shore. The students began to rebuke death, but there was no sign of life. Later, in the hospital, he was pronounced dead. But efforts to revive him continued, along with prayer. God answered the students' prayers, and finally Peter's heart began to beat. He returned to life — with all his faculties intact.

With gratefulness in his heart, Peter determined to serve the Lord. After graduating from CFNI, he went on to get his bachelor's degree, then into the ministry. Today, he is the director of our Caribbean CFNI in Montego Bay with its beautiful dormitories and new 1,000-seat auditorium — the finest conference center in the islands. Pastors bring their youth groups of all sizes for summer camps here. It has become a restoration and revival center.

Chapter Twenty-One

Making Choices

Tom Deuschle, a tall, serious young man came to study at CFNI. When he graduated, he left for Zimbabwe, Africa — a nation then in the throes of a civil war. He ministered there for a couple of years, then returned to Dallas for a time of rest and refreshing.

At the same time, several other male graduates who had been working overseas were on campus checking out "eligible girls." Three young ladies who had attended ORU before coming to CFNI seemed to be the "front runners" in the opinion of the three single male ministers. I watched prayerfully as the "juggling" continued for several months.

Finally, the die was cast: Tom won Bonnie; Larry Hill, now our director of missions after serving in Mexico as a missionary for five years, won Joy; and Marty Nystrom, today a songwriter and music producer, won Jeanie.

Tom returned to Zimbabwe with Bonnie, where they began pastoring. Their church is now the largest in Harare, the capital. They also hold crusades in numerous neighboring nations, with tremendous results. Bonnie is in great demand all over southern Africa as a worship leader, and having four young sons doesn't seem to slow down this energetic couple. Additionally, theirs is no doubt the number one organization feeding and clothing the refugees and those starving due to famines and droughts in the area.

"Call to Me, and I will answer you, and show you great and mighty things, which you do not know" (Jer. 33:3).

Chapter Twenty-Two

Marriages Made in Heaven

Is Christ For The Nations a good place to find a husband or wife if one is single and living a righteous life before God and man? I ask, "What better place?"

At CFNI, permission must be given by a qualified group of our faculty to a couple wanting to become engaged. Weddings cannot take place while the school term is in session.

Our advice to the unmarrieds is: "You have only one choice. It's like going into a jewelry store. Don't pick the first object you see. It may not be a real diamond, but only a zircon. Choose wisely and prayerfully. Remember, it's till death do you part."

Reinhard Bonnke, the German evangelist, has been greatly used of God in massive revivals, especially in Africa. His theme is: Africa shall be saved! Many times he has been targeted for death by the Muslims, but each time God has come to the rescue.

Bonnke's daughter, Gabriella, came to Dallas to attend CFNI. As an attractive, quiet, serious girl, she set a good example for the rest of the students. One day I received a phone call from her father. In a rapid-fire conversation, he told me that his daughter was keeping company with Dario Navac. "What do you know about him? Are there any negatives? She wants to go to Brazil to meet his parents."

I answered him truthfully, "I don't know that much about him. But if there were a problem, I'd have heard about it." The next sound I heard was a click, and I figured he had gotten the information he wanted and had hung up.

When I inquired then about Dario, I learned that his father is the pastor of a large church in Brazil. Dario, the tall, dark and handsome young CFNI student is also a talented singer and piano player.

Bonnke was our commencement speaker when Gabi graduated. Shortly after that, Dario and Gabriella were married. They returned to Brazil for a time, where they had several children. Dario is now traveling with his father-in-law, helping direct his campaigns.

"The LORD is good to those who wait for Him, to the soul *who* seeks Him" (Lam. 3:25).

Chapter Twenty-Three

A CFNI Match

The Boyd McSpaddens had been friends of Gordon's and mine for years. Gary, their son, sang with the "Imperials" and the "Bill Gaither Vocal Band" and was always a fine example for the youth of our nation. I met the McSpaddens again and again at various conventions.

At one particular conference, the McSpaddens told me about their daughter, Cheryl, who had had a great disappointment in her life. At this time, she was searching for God's direction. "Why doesn't she come to Christ For The Nations, attend school and wait for the Lord's leading?" I asked. "Will you speak to her?" they questioned. "Just set up an appointment for lunch and I'll be there," I responded.

They did, and Cheryl and I talked and prayed together. That fall she began attending CFNI.

Cheryl had met Dino Kartsonaikis, the well-known pianist, once before. It so happened, he was based in Dallas at that time. When Dino learned that Cheryl was attending CFNI, he called her. They started dating and before long, they were married. Cheryl, with her lovely voice and natural beauty, has been a real blessing as she works with Dino.

"Witnesses chosen before by God" (Acts 10:41).

Chapter Twenty-Four

A Godly Man is Elected

In 1984, young lawyer Fob James III and his wife, Beth, arrived on the CFNI-Dallas campus with their two small children to attend classes for "one semester." However, they ended up staying on for the next two years.

Fob's father, Fob James Jr., had been governor of the state of Alabama from 1979-1983. His mother, Bobbie, a godly woman, often came to visit her children and grandchildren at CFNI, and she and I became well-acquainted.

Sometimes Bobbie would call me, and we would pray over the phone about a specific need. Her family — strong supporters of Israel — would often host special functions on behalf of Israel.

In 1994, Bobbie called me to pray, along with her family, for God's will concerning Fob James Jr. running again for governor. When the decision to enter the race was made, Bobbie called and asked our student body to pray for success in the campaign. We prayed several times, asking the Lord to lead them step by step.

On election day, November 8, 1994, my son Dennis, his wife, Ginger, and I were in Israel for our annual tour. Excitedly, we sought the results the following morning and finally heard that Fob James Jr. had won the election in Alabama! Shortly afterward, we received invitations to attend the inauguration set for January 16, 1995.

Ginger and I flew together to Alabama. From our hotel, we were driven by a state trooper to the beautiful capitol in the heart of Montgomery and escorted to reserved seats on the platform. In front of us was the large Montgomery Symphony Orchestra which played *Stand Up, Stand Up for Jesus, Onward Christian Soldiers* and other gospel songs. A one-and-a-half hour parade followed, with bands from several Christian schools participating before 25,000 spectators.

It was now time for the inaugural program. Rabbi Elliot Sherman had flown in from Jerusalem. He raised the ram's horn to his lips and blew the shofar. Afterwards, he read from the Bible the portion that says if God's people obey His commands He will bless them. If not, a curse will fall on them.

The Ten Commandments were also read, and special prayers followed. Heather Whitestone, the reigning Miss America from Alabama spoke of her love for Jesus and promised to pray for her governor.

The time came for the oath of office to be taken by the governor-elect. As he took the oath, his six grandchildren laid their hands on the Bible, along with their grandfather, the newly re-elected Fob James Jr., as his wife, Bobbie, their three sons and spouses stood by him. Then he gave his address and concluded with these words:

"Let the Constitution of the United States of America, the greatest formula for freedom struck off by the pen of man since the Magna Carta, stand. Our founding fathers spoke so clearly. Yet for too many years we have watched its original meaning erode away. Long after the sun has set on this beautiful day, let us hope that our descendants can look back on it and say that this was the day when the people set their minds and hearts to return to the principles that served them so well for so long. Thank you and God bless you."

At the conclusion of the governor's speech, the *Lord's Prayer* was sung. A large kosher reception followed. It was a sacred and awesome occasion. Ginger and I felt as if we had just been in a glorious revival.

The following morning, Bobbie called us and about 25 other believers to the governor's mansion, where we gathered to dedicate the James' future residence to the Lord. There we sang and worshiped God as we prayed. I thought afterward, "God, if all 50 U.S. governors honored You like the James' family does, America would be turned around!" Let us pray to that end!

"For the wicked shall not rule the godly, lest the godly be forced to do wrong" (Psa. 125:3 LB).

Christ For The Nations has helped build nearly 10,000 Native Churches (above) Brazilian soliders receiving CFN literature (below).

About 50 million free CFN books were sent overseas (above). CFN sends food, clothing, literature and medical supplies to many needy nations (below).

CFN's Bible school in Minsk, Belarus (above).
CFN's Bible school in Montego Bay, Jamaica (below).

An aerial view of CFN's Bible school in Bad Gandersheim, Germany (above, in upper left corner). CFNI students and staff in Dallas (below).

CFNI-Dallas grad Doug Young with Freda Lindsay in front of his "chapel" he takes to truck stops to witness to drivers (above). Mom Lindsay with camel driver on Mt. of Olives in Jerusalem (below).

Courts of Praise — CFN's greatest financial miracle (above). Sally's Horton's bedroom after the fire that devastated Mary Martha House (below).

The Lindsay family: (back row — left to right) Shira, Ari and Ayal Sorko-Ram; Dennis, Ginger, Missy, Freda, Julia, Shirley and Gilbert Lindsay; (front row) Shani Sorko-Ram; Hawni, Golan, Marcy and Michael Lindsay.

Chapter Twenty-Five

The Grand Finale!

Marceille is a lovable lady who started attending our Sunday afternoon services when we purchased a nightclub in January 1966 and turned it into the Christian Center. She is a Baptist who loves God will all her heart. It wasn't long before she was baptized in the Holy Spirit.

Her husband was Dr. Calvin Harris, a medical physician who practiced in several of the local hospitals. In addition to that career, he was a professor at Southern Methodist University.

Marceille went with us on one of our Israel tours, and we became close friends. At times, I would visit in their home and always received the same "greeting" from Dr. Harris — the cold shoulder. He never attended any of the services with his wife, and he let me know in no uncertain terms that he had no intention of changing. I usually addressed him when I first entered their home, but that was the end of our conversation.

Years went by, and Marceille prayed steadfastly for Calvin. One day, she phoned to tell me Dr. Harris was in the hospital. A number of tests had been run, and the prognosis was not good. Surgery was scheduled, but Calvin had the feeling he wasn't going to make it.

"This could be his time," she said with emotion in her voice. "Can you come?" I assured her I would.

Quickly, I called Dr. Duane Weis, our campus chaplain, and told him of the urgency of the situation. Immediately, we drove to the hospital and were directed to his room. Marceille felt we should see him alone, so she stood outside his room and prayed silently.

Dr. Weis gave Calvin God's simple plan for His so-great salvation — step by step. When he finished, he asked, "Dr. Harris, are you ready to pray the sinner's prayer with me?" The response was, "Yes."

So all three of us prayed that prayer as he opened his heart to God. The joy of the Lord entered his soul, as he proclaimed, "So be it." Marceille then stepped into the room to rejoice with him. Immediately, he wanted his wife to contact their family to tell them what had taken place in his life.

Dr. Harris didn't make it for long after the operation, but he did make it through the Pearly Gates! I was honored to be asked to preach his funeral service to a packed chapel of many local doctors and friends. I told of his conversion at the last hour and encouraged each one to make his peace with God. So be it!

Chapter Twenty-Six

Lacking One Detail

Ron Wahlrobe came to teach at Christ For The Nations. He was all we could ask for: deeply committed to God. A man of integrity. A powerful teacher of the Word. A family man in his 30s with a beautiful wife and two lovely children. Meticulous in his appearance, Ron never had a hair out of place — his clothes were always appropriate for the occasion. He was loved by our students and highly respected by our faculty and staff. A wise steward of his personal business. His car was always waxed and shiny. Near perfect it seemed in every area.

After serving for several years at CFNI, he decided to accept a large pastorate in West Texas. It seemed a great loss to our school, and I was troubled by the move. A couple of times he invited me to his church, including a rally where Bill Bright of Campus Crusade and I were speakers.

Ron invited me to dinner at their newly-built beautiful home. As I expected, the decor was elegant: The furniture, the rugs, the carefully-selected pictures, the colors — everything was coordinated! As he walked me through his home, I thought that this should make any man or woman happy.

One weekend in May, Ron and several of his staff flew in a private plane for an outing in New Mexico. Suddenly, the plane was caught in a downdraft and crashed. Several were injured, but Ron was instantly killed! The news hit our campus like a thunderbolt. Heard again and again was, "It can't be true!" But it was.

No doubt it was even more of a shock to his large congregation and to his wife and two little girls: no husband, no father, no pastor.

Ron had seemingly taken care of every detail in life — except one! He had failed to make a will. That meant all his personal assets were immediately tied up, bringing a hardship to his precious wife and children. When finally the courts settled the estate according to Texas' laws, his wife was required to keep strict records of everything she spent on her children's food, clothing, schooling, etc. and to pay yearly probate costs. None of this would have been necessary if only Ron had made a will.

And this was not the only difficult estate matter that should never have occurred, but several times, with regard to wills, Christ For The Nations, has been involved. No doubt, other ministries could tell of similar situations.

Since the time of its establishment, wills naming Christ For The Nations as a beneficiary have been a tremendous blessing to this ministry. On occasion, it seemed that God alone must surely have been involved in the timing of the disbursement of the funds. For when a great opportunity had arisen for a fruitful investment in an overseas Bible school, a specific Native Church needing funds or an apartment building touching our campus (and one for which our students were praying) suddenly had a "For Sale" sign appear, a check from a will would arrive in our office.

On the other hand, sometimes a will drawn up by a relative or in some way inappropriate, could and has deprived ministries of funds. Such was the case when the largest gift for CFN from a will was delayed. In this will, a certain number of houses were to be sold with CFN receiving the funds. The widow also was to receive a certain number of houses, but had the right to use the funds from the rentals of CFN's portion "until the houses were sold." But no set time was given in which the sale had to be made. So eight years passed during which time, the military base in that city was closed, and also a railroad repair terminal was moved, greatly depreciating the value of the houses.

When Christ For The Nations finally received its part eight years later, instead of receiving $1,250,000, we received about $300,000. We were grateful for what the elderly brother left us, but his intention was to benefit Christ For The Nations much more!

Another case was when a friend and donor of Christ For The Nations for 28 years died naming Billy Graham, the Assemblies of God, Criswell Bible College and Christ For The Nations as her beneficiaries. Her husband had died, they had no children and her brothers were dead.

However, distant family members not named in the will contested it. The case was settled out of court by the parties through a mediator appointed by a local judge. The organizations named in the will did receive the largest portion, but even so it was not the amount intended by the donor.

However, I have learned from these and other experiences that God is our El Shaddai — our provider. How could this ministry have come this far had He not been in control? For surely, this is His work, and He will take care of it.

"And God is able to make all grace abound toward you, that you, always having all sufficiency in all *things* may have an abundance for every good work" (II Cor. 9:8).

Chapter Twenty-Seven

Spared!

I had really looked forward to my trip to Midland, Texas, where I was to be interviewed by Al and Tommie Cooper, owners of Prime Time TV. We had a wonderful evening, and the interview flowed freely. Visiting was Rhonda Coe, who was a teacher at our Jamaican Bible school, as was her husband. She was in the studio with her teenage son and daughter.

After the interview was over, there was discussion as to whether I should be taken to the Plaza Inn in Midland, as this would put me closer to the two churches where I was to speak the next day. Or should I go to the Days Inn in Odessa, which was in the opposite direction, with Rhonda Coe? Finally, it was decided I should go to Midland.

So we climbed into two vehicles; Rhonda, with her daughter in the front seat of her van, and her son in the back. I was escorted to the back seat of the other car. Away we drove with Rhonda saying to me, "I'll see you at the morning service."

The Sunday morning meeting was glorious and the anointing of the Lord was present. But none of the Coes were there. They were at the hospital!

I was told that a large car going about 80 miles an

hour on the highway, driven by a drunk, smashed into Rhonda's van from the rear. The daughter's seat belt broke and her head hit the windshield so hard it made a big indentation in it. Rhonda got a heavy blow in her chest from the steering wheel. Her son was thrown out of the van onto the pavement. The van's back seat ended up in the front seat. The van was totally destroyed.

Fortunately, the Coes suffered no permanent damage, and the van was replaced for a much newer one. Had I been in the van, either in the front or backseat, at my age it could have cost me my life. Praise God, He spared me!

"For He shall give His angels charge over you, to keep you in all your ways. In *their* hands they shall bear you up, lest you dash your foot against a stone" (Psa. 91:11,12).

Chapter Twenty-Eight

"He Calms the Storms"

It was hurricane season in the Caribbean. These storms usually come in the spring and in the fall. They can easily become deadly because of the fierce winds. In some cases, several day's or even a week's notice is possible, depending on the speed and the direction of the storm's forward movement.

At the end of the first week in September 1989, weather reports were coming across the wires that a fierce hurricane was forming in the Caribbean. Since our beautiful campus in Jamaica is right on Montego Bay, we were concerned. Christ For The Nations Institute in Dallas set aside a day of fasting and prayer. We asked our students at the school in Jamaica to join us in prayer for God's protection.

As the days passed, the hurricane winds increased to over two hundred miles per hour and were headed for Jamaica! The faculty, staff and students in Dallas and in Montego Bay stayed in an attitude of prayer.

Finally, the hurricane struck Jamaica! It hit the southern part of the island with force, but lesser winds hit the north where our Bible school is located. Even so, a hotel a stone's throw from our campus was heavily damaged, losing every window. Also, the Holiday Inn was nearly destroyed. It was closed for over a year to make repairs. The Catholic school in the city lost its roof, and our Caribbean CFNI students helped them put on a new one. Though the winds had decreased by the time they hit the northern portion of Jamaica, there was still damage everywhere.

What about our Caribbean Christ For The Nations Institute? We did not lose one single building nor one single window! It was a miracle! An old chicken shack on campus went flying, along with all the chickens, and we lost some trees, which we quickly replaced.

Yes, God did calm the storms over our school in Jamaica, just as He has done many times for us in Dallas when tornadoes have passed over the area. In fact, one recently touched down in Desoto and Lancaster, two suburbs about five miles south of our school, killing several people and doing much damage to the buildings in the town square and dozens of homes were destroyed.

Another time, a hailstorm hit Arlington, about ten miles to our west. It destroyed roofs, windows and thousands of cars, so much so, that one large insurance company is no longer writing policies for that kind of damage. On April 27, 1991, 50 tornadoes were reported in Texas, Oklahoma and Kansas, with 25 deaths. Numbers of times every spring and fall, tornado warnings are issued, but our campus has been spared damage.

God has protected us. "He calms the storm, so that its waves are still. ... Oh, that *men* would give thanks to the LORD *for* His goodness" (Psa. 107:29,31). We do!

Chapter Twenty-Nine

The Writer

Gordon was constantly writing. It seemed so easy for him. Occasionally, he'd work on several books at one time, which made me wonder how he could keep track of where he was in each one. Besides, he was a night owl. He wrote a total of about 250 books of various sizes. He kept me busy typing most of the first drafts and the proofreading of all.

Once a man asked me, "How could one man have written 250 books in one lifetime?" I looked him right in the eyes and replied, "Guess who did all the rest of the work?" — like homeschooling the children when we traveled; when we were settled, taking them to school, to their music lessons, games, Sunday school and church; selecting their clothes; cooking; washing; ironing; keeping an open house for their many friends — to name just a few of my jobs. That was besides working full time at the office.

About ten years after Gordon's death, I noticed that when my two sons, their families and I would spend our annual week of vacation together, Dennis would often work long hours on his computer. I'd ask him, "What are you writing?"

His answer always was, "Wait and see."

One day, he came to me with a question, "Mom, will you do for me what you did for Dad — proofread my books?"

I immediately had misgivings. Does he feel he needs to write because his father was a well-known author? Is he, in fact, a writer? (Not everyone has that particular talent.) What if his books aren't fit to print and won't sell? Besides, he said "books" — plural, and many Christian books are being printed. What if I read one and felt it was not worthy to invest the money needed to print it, and I would need to tell him? Would it so deflate him that he wouldn't be able to rise above it? All of these questions were racing through my mind.

I knew he loved and studied many books on creation science. So when he said, "The subject is going to be creation science," I was somewhat relieved.

"Let's make a deal. I'll proofread the first," I suggested.

I tackled his first book, *Foundations for Creationism*, and as I have sometimes teased when introducing him as President and CEO of Christ For The Nations, I was surprised how much I had taught him!

Recently, a couple, John and Dorothy Hoover, took me to dinner. In the conversation, John, who was a buyer for Western Auto at their main office, said, "I'm taking Dennis' class on Creation. It really ought to be a required class for all of the students. It would establish our youth in God's Word."

Dennis has completed 10 books so far in his Creation Science Series. He still teaches the subject here at CFNI and speaks on it when he travels. His books are also being translated and used in churches and Bible schools overseas. To God be the glory!

"A man's gift makes room for him, and brings him before great men" (Prov. 18:16).

Chapter Thirty

A Change of the Guard

When I reached my 71st birthday, both strangers and friends were anxious to know who would succeed me when I "retired." A board member made a recommendation of a man I had never known nor even heard of. The board member had never heard the man speak. Other suggestions began to surface among some of the faculty who had chosen among themselves.

I felt it was time to take the matter seriously before confusion escalated, so for several weeks, I sought God earnestly. I felt strongly that I should not discuss the matter with anyone, including my family. But I recalled and carefully considered past counsel and opinions ministers had given me concerning the leadership position for the future.

Finally, when our board met for our regularly scheduled meeting on December 14, 1985, I resigned as President of Christ For The Nations. There was silence at first and somewhat of a shock. A motion followed to accept my wishes. The motion passed.

Then I recommended that my youngest son, 39-year-old Dennis Gordon succeed me. The 10-man board voted unanimously for him. At the conclusion of the meeting, the board went directly to the Christmas party for the staff and their families. And when one of the board introduced the new president, the applause for Dennis was tumultuous. Some even stood on chairs and tables in their excitement. Had Gordon been present, I believe he would have approved.

Through the intervening years, I have continued doing much of the work I did previously — speaking in conventions, doing interviews on TV and radio, writing the *World Prayer and Share Letter* two-page monthly article, composing the appeal pages and letters, answering much correspondence, taking overseas trips in behalf of our Bible schools, meeting with some of the 25,000 CFNI grads who return "home" on occasion, having appointments with visiting pastors and missionaries, attending CFNI services on Sundays and Tuesdays — just a few of the responsibilities that fit into my 12-14 hour-long days. To God be the glory!

"The joy of the LORD is your strength" (Neh. 8:10).

Chapter Thirty-One

Our Alumni

Christ For The Nations Institute! Who are the over 25,000 students who have studied here in Dallas these 26 years? Athletes, singers, teachers, musicians, artists, pastors, missionaries, businessmen and women, songwriters, youth and children's workers, retired individuals, doctors, dentists, lawyers, politicians, nurses, housewives. You name it, and you'll find them here.

Linda Zeman, a runner, entered in Fort Worth's 26-mile Cowtown Marathon while she was attending CFNI. An unforeseen event caused her to be two minutes late starting the race. Nonetheless, she won the race by six minutes, setting a new record of 2:45 hours.

****

Bill Francis and his wife worked with Youth With A Mission in El Paso for 10 years after graduating from CFNI. Then he followed his desire to become an Episcopal priest by training at one of their seminaries. Today, he is actively ministering to the Episcopalians in El Paso.

****

Bryan Peterson developed his musical skills further as a student at CFNI and then became worship leader. Here he met Debbie, also musical. Eventually, they were married. When Bryan's father, a pastor for many years in

Madison, Wisconsin became ill, the couple went to Madison to help. Now Bryan and his father pastor the fine church together. Bryan and Debbie's three daughters help, too.

****

Some move into politics. This is the story of two sisters, Lori and Katie Packer, daughters of one of CFN's board members from Detroit. Both, after graduating from CFNI, headed for their state's capital, Lansing, Michigan.

When I visited Lori in her huge office, she was Chief of Staff of the Michigan Senate. And her sister Katie was the Special Assistant to the Senate Majority Leader of the State of Michigan. These two extremely efficient young ladies were in great demand. Lori met a splendid Christian young man, also in politics, whom she married. She is continuing her work as Chief of Staff.

****

Across the border in Ottawa, Canada, is another one of our graduates, Greg Pennoyer. He is also moving up the ladder in his political career.

****

Tammy Loder, whose father, Dr. James Loder, is a professor at Princeton Theological Seminary, attended CFNI. Dr. Loder was our commencement speaker when Tammy graduated. That same week, Tammy married her fiance, Andy. Then they left for overseas to become medical missionaries. Both were university graduates before attending CFNI.

****

As I was walking on our track one morning, I met a tall Russian named Vadim. He told me that while he was in his fifth year of university, majoring in English, an American missionary came to his city needing an interpreter. Vadim heard of the need and decided he would try out his English, while at the same time, earn a little money.

For one month, Vadim interpreted for the missionary. Then came the direct challenge from the missionary: "You need Jesus as your very own Savior."

Vadim replied, "This is a very serious matter. Let me give it some thought for a few days." Moved upon by the Holy Spirit, Vadim returned to the missionary and told him he was ready to ask Jesus to take over his life.

Several months ago, Vadim arrived in the United States, with the help of a friend in America. Here he began looking for a Bible school where he could study. Christ For The Nations Institute was recommended. But how could he pay? He met an unsaved tourist, who gave him $3,000 for his first semester. (Vadim also served at times as a tour guide.) Now this tall Russian is here, busy studying and learning all he can to take the Gospel back to his people.

****

Then, there is 19-year-old, blonde Kirsten, born in Australia. I met her grandparents years ago in Malawi, where they have been missionaries for years. Kirsten's parents are missionaries in Zimbabwe, where Kirsten was involved with youth ministry with her parents, and she won the "B" title (the silver) in the Women's Golf Tournament for Zimbabwe. She came to CFNI to study and to see what God wanted to do in her life.

****

Don and Mary Hilton were both school teachers —

he a teacher of junior high math and she, third-graders. They graduated from Christ For The Nations Institute in Dallas in May 1991 and left for Estonia (a former republic of Russia) a few days later. Both were age 59. This letter arrived in April '96:

"Here's a closer look at some of the things that made it all worthwhile these past four years in Estonia: Eight teachers holding hands while one of them prays before the school day begins; a child taking his/her turn to pray in front of classmates at the beginning or end of the English program for the day; Bible study members, who never prayed until recent years, taking turns praying fluently and with sincerity; comments from the Bible study members thanking us for the teachings about Christian marriage and family; seeing some of our teaching suggestions taking root and being put into practice; seeing teachers' *own* ideas taking root, put into practice and spreading to other classrooms. ...

"Watching teachers answer spiritual questions from children; meeting the children on the street and speaking English with them as their non-English-speaking parents look proudly on; being greeted on the street by people from various churches in town; being greeted with 'Good Morning' (at any time of day or night) by children who know who we are, but are not in the A.C.E. program; hearing the children sing with gusto old songs like *This Little Light of Mine*, *The B-I-B-L-E* and *Jesus Loves the Little Children* — some of them in both English and Russian; listening to teachers share ideas and songs with their colleagues as they meet together monthly in one of the two schools. ...

"One principal's wife (Olga — one of our teachers) saying thanks for the new (modern Russian) Bible that she and her husband (Yuri) are reading together at home; that same principal — the former Komsomol leader in town — telling the parents at a school meeting they should be reading the Bible together at home; a child beaming at us a short time after we prayed for her to be healed of a stomachache.

"Watching new teachers slowly changing from skeptics to believers as they work with the Christian school materials, with believing colleagues, and attend Bible studies; a father wanting his child in A.C.E. so badly he spends many summer days collecting berries in the forest to sell at the farmers' market; Anya and Marina — little friends of one A.C.E. girl who has moved to Russia — come to our apartment nearly every week to play games and read the Bible, though they aren't in our classes; 10-year-old Andrei, a brilliant fourth grader who has trouble doing his work — his mind is elsewhere for obvious reasons: his father was imprisoned for a murder he committed last year; Misha and his daughter, Sveta, from the Islamic southern republic of Tajikistan, coming to Bible study each week though they don't profess to believe in Christ (but are more open each week).

"Thank you, Lord, for these and many more reasons."

"He who continually goes forth weeping, bearing seed for sowing, shall doubtless come again with rejoicing, bringing his sheaves *with him*" (Psa. 126:6).

Chapter Thirty-Two

Reaching the Top

In 1987, Scott Appleton gave us the following testimony:

"In 1963, I made it to the top. I was the number one football player on the number one team in the nation. Our team had won the first national championship at the University of Texas. Then, for icing on the cake, I made All American and received the Outland Award as outstanding lineman in the country. I thought to myself, 'It can't get any better than this.'

"It did get better: I was drafted in the first round by the Dallas Cowboys and the Houston Oilers. I told my mother, 'I've got it made. I am going to make a million dollars and get to stay in Texas.'

"During the five years of professional football (three with Houston and two with the San Diego Chargers), I had everything a person is supposed to have to be happy in America: a lot of money, a big house, Cadillacs, a beautiful wife and daughter, and my picture on bubble gum cards.

"The only thing missing in my life was happiness. I was miserable, so I tried to fill the emptiness with alcohol. My plan to make a million dollars on the stock market failed, and I went from having a fortune to being in debt in just a few months. I also lost my job as a football player and my family by divorce.

"I ended up in the state hospital in Austin, Texas, just a few miles from the university where I was cheered and thought of as a hero. I was in the 'nut house' in Austin that I had been afraid to go near as a child.

"The time had come in my life when there was no more playing games with God. I began to beg, 'God, please help me.' I finally got into a Bible study for a few months, and the miracle occurred. I was delivered from alcohol addiction — Jesus had set me free indeed!

"I'm happy now. I have purpose and direction, and the Spirit of God is teaching me how to love others and to let them love me. I'm finally a winner — not because of myself, but because of my Savior, Jesus Christ."

Scott Appleton attended Christ For The Nations Institute in 1986-87. When he left Dallas, he began working with a Christian organization. He continued serving the Lord until he died of a heart attack in 1992. He had made preparation with God for that day that comes to everyone. He had taken advantage of God's provision for salvation.

"If we confess our sins, He is faithful and just to forgive us *our* sins" (I Jn. 1:9).

Chapter Thirty-Three

Praying for the Pope

One day, a couple concluding their studies at CFNI came to tell me that they felt God was calling them to start a church in Rome — close to the Vatican, so they could pray for the pope.

With 25,000 students having attended CFNI in the past 26 years, it wasn't the first time one of them had come to me to tell me of a pipedream. Usually, I would say little, pray with them for God's will to be done in their lives and direct them according to His promise in Psalm 16:11: "You will show me the path of life."

Sometimes, I would shake my head in disbelief after the person was gone. Such was my feeling, to be truthful, when Marty and Cathy Lombardo came to my office. But it turned out, I was totally wrong in their case!

The couple did go to Rome and witnessed wherever there was an open door. Several years went by, and they faithfully did what they could.

Then, God laid it on Marty's heart to go each morning to the Vatican Square. This is the place where hundreds of thousands gather when the pope speaks. Marty was to arise between 2-6 a.m., whatever time God awakened him. He was to dress up in a suit and necktie, go to the Square, kneel down and pray out loud for an hour or longer for the pope and the Catholic people. This he did — until Vatican police came to move him on, asking brusquely, "What are you doing here?"

"I'm praying."

"Who gave you permission?"

"The Holy Father," replied Marty. And with that answer, the guard left and Marty continued to pray each day.

A second miracle happened when the beautiful Methodist Church on the Vatican Square right across from the pope's residence was offered to the Lombardos for 20 years. For the first 10 years, they could use the church rent-free. Negotiations would be underway for the other 10 years.

Since the facility has several stories, the Lombardos live there and have room for guests on special occasions. When our tour came through Rome from Israel, we worshiped with the Lombardos' congregation, taking part in the services. Also, wouldn't you know, the Lombardos served all 22 of our tour group with tasty Italian spaghetti in their living room.

God has provided a place of worship in the heart of Rome.

"Oh, worship the LORD in the beauty of holiness!" (I Chron. 16:29).

Chapter Thirty-Four

CFNI Pastors

The faculty and I have watched 25,000 students come and go in the past 26 years since CFNI began. One of the joyful rewards of our labor among them is to see the quality pastors raised up by God.

Rev. Michael Massa is one such leader. His older brother, Mark, a noble young man, attended CFNI first. Then, as Andrew in the Bible, "He first found his own brother Simon (Peter), and said to him, 'We have found the Messiah.' ... And he brought him to Jesus" (Jn. 1:41,42).

So Michael, a Baptist and a graduate of Tennessee Technological University came to Dallas and graduated from CFNI. For several years now, he has been pastoring Church of the King, one of Dallas' finest congregations.

Here is a letter Michael wrote to me: "CFNI was the place where the Lord revealed Himself to me in worship, planted the vision for world harvest in my heart, began to equip me for spiritual warfare, instructed me in the message of faith, placed a continual yearning for the release of the gifts of the Spirit in our day as in years gone by, and most importantly, began to build the priority of prayer as 'a business in my life.'

"In addition, He directed me to my wife, joined us

together with friendships for ministry that cross international boundaries that I believe will bear fruit eternally, and deposited much of the vision for ministry that is in my heart today.

"Further, there was the faith you had in the Lord to allow me to minister there and to travel with you on tours. It is a privilege from the Lord which I thank Him for on a regular basis."

Another graduate of whom we are proud is Mihai Dumitrascu from Romania. Mihai, the son of a pastor, recently wrote from Galati, Romania:

"Greetings to you in the Name of the Lord Jesus Christ! It is a pleasure for me to remember the time spent at CFNI. I graduated in December 1992, and after that, I came to Romania. In March 1994, I became the pastor of Pentecostal Temple in Galati. Together with children and adults, there are 1,000 members in the church, and it is growing every day. Praise God for it."

****

Just recently, I received the following letter from alumni John Hollar, pastor of Tree of Life Church in San Angelo, Texas:

"Ann and I have seen the Lord do marvelous things over the past 20 years since our arrival at Christ For The Nations. When we graduated in 1978, we went back to our hometown in Oklahoma where we built a new home. I was working on the Santa Fe railroad and had plenty of money. We finished the house and lived in it for two years when the Lord directed us to sell our house, quit the railroad and move to San Angelo. Bob Long was pastoring a church in San Angelo and he needed me to come to be his youth pastor. Bob and I had been friends at CFNI. This proved to be the most important connection to launching us into full-time ministry.

"Because of my CFNI background, I desperately wanted our church to have a strong missions emphasis. Since that time, we have operated by faith to see the Lord open the first A.C.E. Christian school in Moscow through my school principal, Brad and his wife, Irene.

"We have seen through our ministry 11 pastors placed in ministry, four new churches started and many missionaries both long-term and short-term placed in countries such as Morocco, the Philippines, Guatemala, Chile, Spain, Russia, Arab Emirates and Mexico.

"One thing I have tried to instill in all the pastors I have sent out is that they should have a missions emphasis. We believe the missions director ought to be the first person on staff next to the pastor. He may wear a few other hats but his primary purpose should be to focus on outreach to the nations.

"The church here is a strong congregation of over 500 people in attendance on Sundays with an A.C.E. Christian school of a 120 students. We have owned this present facility for six years, and we will be burning the note on May 19.

"Recently, a family in our church donated us six acres on the west side of town to build new facilities. This property is valued at $265,000, and we start construction on a new 1,200-seat auditorium in the near future. God has been so good to provide for us in abundance."

****

Here's another letter I just received from alumnus

Robert Bogard who is the executive pastor at Resurrection Life Full Gospel Church in Grandville, Michigan:

"It has been three years since I left CFNI to come on staff here in Grandville. It has been a great three years, to say the least. I wanted to take a moment and share with you the heritage we draw from in relation to the school.

"Our staff consists of Pastor Duane VanderKlok and wife, Jeanie ('76 grads), my wife, Rose and me ('76 grads), Scott Vruggink and his wife, Jackie ('86 grads), Jon and Jennifer Grossi ('92 and '93 grads), Curt and Jennifer Coffield ('92 grads), and another associate pastor's wife is a '79 grad.

"In the past three years, we have interned four graduates of CFNI's Third-Year Youth ministry program (three of which we have placed in ministry). At present, we have three Third-Year Youth grads working with us. As well, we have approximately 10 students attending CFNI in Dallas with 10-15 more planning to attend beginning this fall.

"Our church has grown under Pastor Duane's leadership from 300 in 1983 to a Sunday morning attendance of 2,800. In the past three years that I have been here, we have grown from 1,500 to our present attendance. We have a night Bible school that averages about 40 students. Our school has just completed its third year, and we will graduate 12 students in June.

"This is just a short sketch of the affect CFNI has had on this part of the globe. May God continue to richly bless you and the ministry in Dallas and the world."

So it is with the several thousand CFNI alumni who are pastoring churches large and small, at home and abroad. They will receive a big reward for their labors from the Lord.

"And there are also many other things that Jesus did, which if they were written one by one, I suppose that even the world itself could not contain the books that would be written" (Jn. 21:25).

Chapter Thirty-Five

A Heartbreak!
A Family Redirected

He sang at our *Voice of Healing* conventions in the late '40s and early '50s. Nobody could forget him. His wife was an organist and a real asset to him. The couple traveled with their small son from meeting to meeting.

But in those days, income was small for preachers, and often less for singers. And back then, there were no tapes or videos to sell, so few gospel singers survived. Bars and nightclubs paid better, so this robust vocalist left his family for the nightlife. Shortly after, one of their three sons was killed in a car accident.

The wife (we'll call her Mary) did the best she could to earn a living for her two sons. The eldest of the boys, Jim (also an assumed name), would sit on the front row while his mother played the organ at church. Never had I seen such a young child (about 8 years old) worship the Lord so seriously.

After several years in Dallas, Mary remarried and the family moved to Austin where they attended church regularly. Jim was now 12. His Sunday school teacher took a real "interest" in him and on occasions, would take him home during the weekend.

This teacher selected three other boys, invited them to his home one at a time. With these four boys, he formed a "private club," telling them they were very special. He instructed them not to speak to anyone about this club — their parents, their friends, no one. You guessed it: The Sunday school teacher was a homosexual!

It turned out that Jim, the robust, good-looking young teenager had a tremendous singing voice like his delinquent, absentee birth-father. And a talent, like his mother, to play the piano, organ and keyboard.

Jim later married a very beautiful, talented girl and fathered a son and a daughter. It seemed he had the secret homosexuality under control. Jim moved about in Christian circles, using his tremendous talents. For a period, he was on the music staff at our Bible school.

At length, some of his actions began to cause problems. He left CFN and took a leadership role in the music department of a large church. Finally, while employed there, he was arrested twice one summer by undercover agents in the restrooms of two different city parks as he solicited the agents for homosexual purposes. Because no previous charges had ever been filed against him, he was released to his lovely family.

He moved to another large city, where he again worked for a church, again in the field of music. When his sin was discovered, he moved to another state, where a large church hired him for his tremendous musical ability.

Several years later, he was diagnosed as being HIV+. A divorce followed. He then returned to Texas.

A few times he phoned me at the office. I could not bring myself to talk to him, until finally one day, I accepted his call and made an appointment. When he arrived, he was so gaunt, I hardly recognized him — that former fine-looking boy I had known and loved as a child.

He agreed to let me interview him on tape for over an hour, as he told me the whole sad story. By now, he had full-blown AIDS. We prayed together, and it was not long after that he died. I was one of the two speakers at his funeral, where I watched his family sitting on the front row weeping bitterly. A life that could have done so much for God had ended so tragically and so early.

His wife has since married a fine Christian, and the entire family is serving God. The daughter has attended some of our youth programs at CFNI — a lovely young lady. God has picked up the pieces of their broken lives and is using them for His glory!

"Surely He has borne our griefs and carried our sorrows. ... But He was wounded for our transgressions, He *was* bruised for our iniquities; the chastisement for our peace was upon Him, and by His stripes we are healed" (Isa. 53:4,5).

Chapter Thirty-Six

Dogsledding

Alaska! All my life I dreamed of going there — that enchanting snow-white land of peace and calm.

So when one day I received an invitation to speak at a women's conference outside of Anchorage, I was elated. Usually, I pack a few hours before I leave on a trip, but this one was different. I had a lot to pack. Long johns, wool socks, fur-lined boots, sweaters, scarfs, a fur hat, mittens — the whole bit. I was ready early.

I had planned to fly to Anchorage on February 27, but due to some obligations, changed my ticket to the 28th. When I did arrive in Anchorage, I heard that a volcano had erupted on the 27th, closing the airport and covering the city with a coat of volcanic ash.

Two ladies, Debbie and Shelley, picked me up and drove me to Little Beaver Camp. One lane of the highway had been cleared, but the snow was piled so high on both sides of the road, we could see nothing as we drove along.

This had been Alaska's heaviest winter snow. The animals were having to be fed by the government's dropping bales of hay along the way. Many of the moose were being killed by trains as they were foraging for food on the railroad tracks. The railroad engineers would notify the city officials, who in turn, would pick up the dead animals and use them for several purposes.

With all the heavy snow, I wondered whether women would be able to make it to the conference. About one hundred were present. One carload drove a couple hundred miles — to my astonishment. These women had sacrificed greatly to come. They were about the most receptive and hungry group to whom I have ever had the privilege to minister. About 20 were baptized in the Holy Spirit, and several were healed. It was a three-day convention, and they had me speaking three times a day. It was glorious!

Then I went back to Anchorage, where I spoke on Sunday at Willow Chapel, with Missionary Bill Pepper. Would anybody come in the almost continuous snowstorm? The church was packed, and the service which started at 11 a.m., lasted until 2:30 p.m. Many received the Holy Spirit.

The next morning, my hostess asked me, "Would you like to go dogsledding?"

Before I realized what I was saying, I replied, "Why not?"

Immediately, the couple called friends of theirs who were dog-breeders. And I was on my way, all dressed up in my warm paraphernalia, including some things my hostess added.

By the time we arrived, I was a little intimidated. I am never one to back down, so I listened to the instructions and put on my "seat belt." Away we went, flying through the snow — fun, but scary! Only once did I fall halfway off of my sled. God protected me — even on the dogsled!

When I returned home, I was teased by several who suggested, "Why didn't you just stay in Anchorage and volunteer for the annual Iditarod Dogsledding Competition?" I decided that wasn't my calling.

"For wisdom *is* better than rubies, and all the things one may desire cannot be compared with her" (Prov. 8:11).

Chapter Thirty-Seven

Khartoum, Sudan Trip

While visiting two refugee camps in Khartoum, Sudan, East Africa several years ago, I saw the most heartrending sights of my entire life.

It took two days of going from one government office to another to get permits to enter the camps. Additional time was well-spent checking out individuals and agencies with whom we had been involved back home. Then the time came to visit the camps in southern Sudan, where Ethiopian Christians fleeing from the harsh communist regime in Ethiopia had taken refuge.

We got up at 4 a.m., for we wanted to get an early start for the 400-mile round-trip. Shortly after 5 a.m., four of us climbed into the cab of a pickup truck: David, our driver (a young British man, age 20); Laurel, a young woman from Canada — both relief volunteers; Norman Young (CFN's business administrator and my nephew by marriage); and I.

A heavy dust storm had blown in during the night, and it was completely blotting out the sun. After joining our hands in prayer, we started out on our never-to-be-forgotten journey. We drove mile after mile, bumping along on roads built by the United States, China and Yugoslavia, we saw a seemingly endless desert of sand

and dust. Not a single blade of grass.

Carcasses of camels, mules, donkeys, cows and sheep were strewn along the barren, parched sand. No water. No food. The bodies of refugees who had died had obviously been picked up. But the vultures — scavengers — quickly found the animal carcasses, swooped down upon them and gorged themselves.

We saw a few herd of emaciated cattle and camels standing in groups on the open, dry desert — so thin, it seemed their legs wouldn't hold them. The animals that appeared to fare best in this battle for survival were the large herd of wiry, skinny goats. They were eating every bit of sagebrush they could find. The land had already been denuded of its forests. Every tree had been cut down and used for firewood.

About 10:30 a.m., we approached the first refugee camp: We were surrounded by friendly children of every age. They were all in filthy rags, many with colds, runny noses and watering eyes. Oh, how they all chattered — in a language we couldn't understand. Each wanted to hold our hands and to be loved. They were everywhere, and they followed us wherever we walked.

The "homes" were mostly makeshift straw shelters. The more fortunate had been assigned a small canvas tent.

We visited the "hospital" — a thatched roof with sides open to allow escape of the unbearable stifling heat of 100° or more. (The sun had by now long since broken through the clouds as we had journeyed south.)

The sights I saw shall forever remain with me! At the entrance to the hospital, on a crude refugee-built cot, lay a child of a year or so dying of dysentery. His private parts were covered with a clump of filthy rags. A "nurse" was catching in a piece of plastic, the green secretion coming from his little body. His glassy eyes never moved. Though his face and body were covered with flies, he was too weak to shoo them away.

A woman trying to nurse a tiny orphan of about five pounds, was waving one hand back and forth, attempting to keep the flies from the boy's face — but it was hopeless.

From cot to cot we went, each case seeming worse than the one before — men and women whose bodies were so emaciated we could count every rib. Children who had lost one parent, or both, dying of starvation, dehydration, malaria, pneumonia or whatever.

The tuberculosis ward was full. A woman sat dejectedly on the ground with her child of eight pounds or so. The nurse told us that both the mother and the baby had TB. Men were coughing violently. Children of all ages — a rack of bones — too weak to sit up or ever stand again, short of a miracle. Several times, I could no longer hold back my tears. I had never seen such human misery! I said aloud, "God, why don't You start all over again? Man has made such a mess."

Why all this suffering? Most of the over one million refugees in Sudan come from Tigray. This Ethiopian province of about five million is 80% Christian. (Three million will slowly starve to death.) Many of the women and children have fled to Sudan, walking 10-15 days to reach refugee camps.

Left behind in the near-ghost villages are the old, the

sick, and sometimes widowed mothers with small children. The Ethiopian government would not allow food from the United States, Europe, Britain and elsewhere to be taken to the Tigrayans. Most is taken instead for its own army. One agency we're working with is nonetheless bringing food from Sudan to feed these "left-behinders" to keep them from certain starvation.

Another problem for most of Africa is that at the time of our trip, there had been the severest drought in 30 years. An agricultural engineer we met, who had worked in Africa for 12 years, gave us encouraging information: He pointed out that Central Canada gets only 10 inches of rain annually and grows fine crops. Africa, even the Sahara, gets 18 or more inches.

He said under his team's supervision, even with much less rain, good crops were growing and erosion was being stopped. Teams were beginning to educate the farmers. They planned to plant trees to help increase rainfall.

Permanent refugee camps are not a solution; only getting to the root of the problem will make the people self-sufficient. The Sahara Desert need no longer spread its long tentacles over the African farmlands. It can be stopped, but it will take time and determination.

In the camps we visited, food and water were given priority. The basic foods passed out were grains, powdered skim milk and high protein biscuits. The filthy rags the children and adults were wearing made it apparent to us that no money was left for clothes. Those few who had even a ragged, dirty blanket were among the fortunate. And when winter comes, the desert gets very cold at night.

Christ For The Nations is sending tons of donated food to the starving in several critical areas of the world, paying only for the shipping costs.

Today, great hostility is coming against Christians in southern Sudan by the Muslim government. Persecution, imprisonment and death are the lot of many believers. And slavery is being revived, according to *Readers Digest* (3/96). The Muslim Arabs who control the north are the chief perpetrators. They are after southern Sudan's fertile land, untapped oil and mineral reserves. The Dinka people (the largest tribe), who are Christians or practice native religion, live in the south. The Arab invaders storm into their villages, seize the cattle and go from hut to hut gathering grains, blankets, salt, etc. Then they round up the men, women and children. Anyone trying to escape is beaten, mutilated and murdered.

Of the million people in the area, only about 200,000 remain at liberty. The rest are either dead, exiled, abducted into slavery or deported. The slaves are being exported to Libya, Chad, Mauritania or the Persian Gulf states. The men are murdered for any resistance. The women and girls are abused and raped before and after they are sold at the slave markets. Little boys as young as 6 years are used to supply blood to the Sudanese military. And yet there has been no worldwide protest against this horrific slave trade. Pray that God will intervene in this desperate situation.

"The harvest truly is great, but the laborers are few; therefore pray. ... Blessed is the nation whose God is the LORD" (Lk. 10:2; Psa. 33:12).

Chapter Thirty-Eight

The "Laughing Revival"

Steve Strang, editor of *Charisma*, wrote me, asking for my opinion of the "Laughing Phenomenon" breaking out in the world. Here is what I told him:

I've often been asked this by our students and others, "What's with the 'Toronto Blessing'?" I've attended John Arnott's meetings in Toronto, Dallas and Jerusalem and read *Catch the Fire* by Guy Chevreau and recently, *The Father's Blessing* by John Arnott himself (which I recommend).

This dancing, laughing, "strange" revival is not altogether new to me. For I recall when my late husband, Gordon, and I pastored the Ashland, Oregon Assembly of God in the '40s, something "unusual" happened. The church had 40 members when we arrived. Several were teachers and professionals since Ashland had a college, and it was located a few blocks from our church. Our people loved God but were very proper. No emotion.

Gordon asked Rev. John Stiles, who we were told had a Holy Ghost ministry, to come for a revival. When Stiles wrote us that he would accept, we were astonished when we read his postcard. His grammar and spelling were atrocious! Gordon "warned" our congregation of his "lacks," but admonished the people to receive him warmly. They did.

Soon our church was packed, and many who came from far and near were filled with the Spirit. One Lutheran man, Karl Oeser, owned a garage and gasoline station on Main Street near our church. His wife was a devout Christian; he never came. But the reports of the revival interested him, so he began attending.

At the close of a particularly glorious night, while Karl was sitting like a statue — his usual posture, he suddenly jumped to his feet and ran full speed the entire length of our church.

I was horrified as I watched, and I remember thinking that one of two things had to happen: When Karl hit the wall, God would have to make a hole in it for him to get through, or he would injure or kill himself! Neither happened! When Karl hit the wall, he did a flip in the air and ran back full speed in the opposite direction, speaking in tongues! Such Holy Ghost laughter resulted, as the whole congregation basked in God's glory and presence. And the Oesers became one of our most faithful families!

Then I recall that in the '50s, every time a revival came to Oak Cliff Assembly in Dallas, old Sister Stanley would dance up and down in the aisles. Her bun would fall from the top of her head, and her hairpins would scatter on the floor, as she laughed, cried and spoke in tongues. The rest of us just watched and enjoyed it.

In the '60s, Costa Deir came to our city and with him, the dancing. Then in the '70s, with Kenneth Hagin came the laughing. More recently, laughter broke out among our students when Cindy Jacobs ministered for a week, and again when Joyce Meyers spoke at our women's conference. "Carpet time" — as Arnott calls it — followed.

Now it is becoming almost common to hear that this outpouring of God's Spirit is taking place in nations around the world.

What about the "excesses" as some would call them? Yes, there will be excesses in any mighty revival. During the Great Awakening under Jonathan Edwards, many religious leaders rejected it and called it the "Great Clamour." In fact, Edwards himself wrote of "great imprudences and irregularities of conduct."

John Arnott asked, "Is it demonic, the flesh or the Holy Spirit?" It has to be one of the three. And that's why we need ministers who operate in the gifts of the Spirit and have discerning of spirits, lest we miss God. For as Gordon used to say, "Stay open to God's move. Extremes will wash themselves out."

This big move of God is the first we've seen in 40 years. When our group drove to the auditorium in Canada where the "Toronto Blessing" is taking place (my first visit), we had a difficult time finding a parking space. I remarked, "For 2,500 people to be at church at 7:00 p.m. on a Saturday night without a 'special feature,' something must be taking place here." And there was!

My son-in-law and daughter, Ari and Shira Sorko-Ram had booked John Arnott for three days at the Holiday Inn in Jerusalem. The meetings began the week of Prime Minister Yitzhak Rabin's assassination. What seemed like an unlikely time for a revival to begin — let alone in Israel — turned out to be divine planning. The auditorium was packed with 800 guests, and God moved.

How do we judge a revival? By its results. And in these meetings, thousands of lives are being moved upon by God. In England, a nation that had almost died spiritually, 5,000 to 7,000 churches are now on fire for God.

Now this question faces each of us: Is this the end-time revival Joel prophesied is coming and for which we've all been praying and waiting? If so, we better move with it. Fear and pride can keep us from it.

We're seeing the "falling away" that the Bible also prophesied was coming. What did Sodom and Gomorrah do that America and many nations aren't doing or even surpassing — considering the great light with which we have been blessed?

No, we'll never completely understand God's ways and methods. Neither did those who lived and walked with Him in Bible days. Let's keep our hearts open and our ears tuned to His leading. For God is moving rapidly to gather in His harvest through Benny Hinn, Reinhard Bonnke, T.D. Jakes, the Promise Keepers, Rodney Howard-Browne, John Arnott and many others. Let's stay spiritually alert!

"Obey My voice, and I will be your God, and you shall be My people. And walk in all the ways that I have commanded you, that it may be well with you" (Jer. 7:23).

Chapter Thirty-Nine

Our Greatest Financial Miracle

Gordon, our three grown children and I were looking for a location in Dallas to build the headquarters of Christ For The Nations. With and without real estate agents, we looked and prayed. Finally, all five of us agreed on one area.

The choice was providential. Today our campus covers 75 acres, touches two of Dallas' busiest freeways, and is only seven minutes south of downtown Dallas. That there were several apartment houses in close proximity to the first building we purchased turned out to be an added blessing to us as we were able to purchase and pay for them one at a time instead of having to build them, raise funds and lose precious time.

Touching the southern end of our campus, a private corporation had built 152 nice brick apartments with one, two and three bedrooms. The land was nicely landscaped and tall trees graced the place, called Fawn Ridge West. Approximately 10 years ago, the owner went into bankruptcy and the government repossessed these apartments.

Low income families, subsidized by the government, arrived. Later, two gangs moved in. Each Saturday night, we'd hear what sounded like firecrackers going off on the Fourth of July. But they weren't firecrackers; they were real bullets!

The *Dallas Morning News* carried several pages with color-pictures, calling this the worst crime area in the city.

Several years passed, and the violence worsened. It was then the owners of Fawn Ridge West apartments offered to sell them to Christ For The Nations. Since they are located on 11 acres of land across the street from a part of our campus, it seemed logical for us to buy them. There was only one problem: We did not have the money to make the purchase; so we turned down the offer.

In 1995, we were approached by the governmental agency operating the units. Five of us met with them. After several hours of negotiations, we offered them a very small amount. This time, they turned us down!

A few weeks later, we received word that they were ready to sell us the apartments at the unbelievably low price — they are worth millions! We voted to buy them. So now Christ For The Nations is the owner of an additional 152-brick apartments. We have named them Courts of Praise.

We'll have plenty of apartments for our students and our alumni, who often want to work on degrees at other local Christian colleges after they finish their time at CFNI. These apartments will also provide space for those wanting to live on campus and be a part of our 24-hour-a-day prayer ministry as soon as our World Missions Center, now under construction, is completed.

All of the buildings in the "new" apartment complex have new roofs, and the main air conditioning unit is new. The streets have recently been black-topped, and a fine iron security fence has been built around the entire property.

Surely, this is our greatest financial miracle, and we give God all the glory.

However, we are constrained by the terms of the contract to make the considerable repairs that are needed. At this writing, we have renovated half of the 152 apartments, and they are occupied as soon as completed. Some 40 people are on a waiting list. No wonder. The nine units of Courts of Praise are the loveliest apartments on campus.

"The LORD is with you while you are with Him. If you seek Him, He will be found by you; but if you forsake Him, He will forsake you" (II Chron. 15:2).

Chapter Forty

A Millionaire Phones Me

I first met this millionaire (we'll call him Ray) about 20 years ago. He once came to one of our banquets and sponsored three Native Churches.

Both he and his older brother were inventors — geniuses, industrialists. His two plants covered about two city blocks. He and his family lived on his estate in an eight-bedroom house.

When he and his wife picked me up in Detroit at the Full Gospel Businessmen's Conference after I had spoken at the women's luncheon, they drove me to the airport in their sleek, long limousine.

On the way, he showed me the fine looking church he had built for himself, but lamented, "I couldn't even get my children to attend (he was the preacher) so I sold it."

Ray took his family on a round-the-world trip and when they arrived in Israel, they stayed in one of the finest hotels for about a month. He was born of a Jewish mother. While in Israel, he did not invest in his youngest brother's ministry — who has been in the work of the Lord there for a long time.

Several years ago, Ray and his wife arrived on campus in their custom-built motor home. Ray himself had designed and built it; it was entirely automatic, a showpiece. One businessman told me, "A half-million couldn't touch it."

Ray hooked up the motor home to an outlet we had on campus, and when he left after several days, he gave me a check for $31.80, "for the use of electricity."

Last summer, Ray called me. "How are things going, Freda?"

"Fine."

"What's new?" he asked.

Then I told him about the miracle God had given us in allowing us to purchase the 152 Courts of Praise apartments. I told him that all we needed now was money to restore them as they were heavily damaged on the inside, but would end up being the most beautiful part of our 75-acre campus when repaired.

"Ray, we need them badly. Would you like to help us?" I asked.

Slowly came his answer: "Freda, you know me. I always have my own projects. I'm here right now in North Carolina with my two sons. I've just completed building my retirement home. Besides, I've bought a whole island here that I'm going to develop and erect some beautiful homes on," and on and on he went with his money-making schemes.

Shortly after, Hurricane Felix was barreling up the East Coast and was supposed to hit North Carolina and Virginia with a frenzy. Ray had just purchased a speedboat and a fancy yacht. So he said to his son, "I'm going out to secure the speedboat. I believe the yacht is safe in the marina."

Out he went to where the speedboat was anchored — a couple hundred feet from his new home. Several people on shore were watching Ray, as he got into the boat, started the motor, leaned over the side as if he were picking up something and fell into the water. Down into the water he went, but in a moment he came to the surface, calling for help. A bit later, he disappeared again in the water and this time, he didn't come up.

The bystanders alerted the police, and for three days, the search continued. When they finally found his body, it was under the speedboat in six feet of water, a couple of hundred feet from his home. (He was well over six feet tall.)

The search team had thought his body was washed out to sea — away from the shore. They were wrong. And Hurricane Felix never did make shore in North Carolina or Virginia! It had passed this area and gone out to sea. Ray had died in his fifties — unnecessarily!

The Bible does remind us: "It is appointed for men to die once, but after this the judgment" (Heb. 9:27). How wise it is for us to "stay ready" to meet our Creator. I John 2:15 says, "Do not love the world or the things in the world. If anyone loves the world, the love of the Father is not in him." And as I have heard Wayne Myers say, "You never see a hearse pulling a U-Haul trailer."

Some have time to make plans for eternity, but because they are ignorant of the Bible and spiritual matters, they neglect to prepare their souls by asking Jesus to forgive their sins — the only key to heaven.

I recall when our tour visited Moscow, our Christian guide took us to see Nikita Khrushchev's grave — in a

Christian cemetery! He was not to be buried in Red Square with the former communist dictators. He asked to be buried in the Christian cemetery — the Russian Orthodox Cemetery — and he was!

Then there was King Charles the Great — Charlemagne — of France who lived from 742-814. Charles had wanted to conquer the world. He made elaborate preparation for his homegoing. He built for himself a large mausoleum — big enough to hold his throne. He asked to be seated on it after his decease and to have his crown placed on his head. All these instructions were carried out.

Years later, permission was granted for a team to open the mausoleum. Many valuables were found. There still sat the skeleton of Charlemagne on his throne. Only now, his crown had slipped down and encircled his bony neck. On his lap was a book — The Book — the Bible. Charlemagne's finger pointed to the verse: "What will it profit a man if he gains the whole world, and loses his own soul?" (Mk. 8:36). A mighty important question with no positive answer.

Chapter Forty-One

From Death to Life

It was October 1992. Dennis and Ginger had just arrived in Argentina after a 36-hour plane trip and were immediately taken to a speaking engagement that Sunday night. I had just concluded our Christ For The Nations banquet in Cincinnati, Ohio; the six other members of our group went for supper, while I had a cup of soup in my room and went to bed early. Scarcely had I fallen asleep when the phone rang, startling me.

A friend was calling to tell me that 17-year-old Missy, my granddaughter and Dennis and Ginger's eldest child, had just been struck by a hit-and-run driver. "What is her condition? Is she alive?" I asked. This friend didn't know.

My mind seemed blank. After a few moments, I called the Dallas hospital closest to our campus, telling them who I was and asked for any information about my granddaughter, Missy Lindsay. The operator said, "She's been taken to Methodist Hospital. That's all I know."

Quickly, I phoned that hospital. When I was able to contact Missy's other grandmother, Mildred, I breathed a short sigh of relief. Then I anxiously asked, "Is Missy alive?"

When she answered, "Yes," I began to praise God.

"What happened?" was my next question. Here is what she told me:

"Missy was on her way to the campus cafeteria in Gordon Lindsay Tower (the former Sheraton) for a Sunday evening snack with other students. The signal light was green as she stepped from the curb. But a speeding Cadillac, racing at about 50 mph to make the light, hit Missy, threw her on the hood, carried her for a distance, and then spilled her onto the pavement — without stopping.

"Several minutes later an officer pronounced her 'dead at the scene of the accident.' But the students immediately surrounded her as she bled from the back of her head, calling her back to life. An ambulance rushed her to the hospital, with the students continuing in prayer.

"She has now regained consciousness and is crying and asking for her mother," said Mildred.

Needless to say, I rejoiced! Dennis and Ginger were called, and advised to return immediately. After prayer, they decided to finish their scheduled week of meetings in Argentina.

On the third day, two medical doctors came into Missy's room. One of them said to her, "Missy, go home and be a good girl. You should be dead! You're dismissed from this hospital!" It was truly a miracle of God.

Missy spent the next two years at Christ For The Nations Institute, then continued her education at Oral Roberts University. To God be the glory!

"But the very hairs of your head are all numbered. Do not fear therefore; you are of more value than many sparrows" (Matt. 10:30,31).

Chapter Forty-Two

Friends Indeed

Oh, how important friends have been to me, especially these last 23 years. Often, a phone call from one of them lifts me up.

Such friends are Chris and Margaret Dornbierer — a Swiss family that immigrated to America with their two children. Chris began working in a greenhouse in New Jersey where he learned much about flowers, plants, plant care and trade.

Finally, he bought 500 acres in the Pennsylvania hills and turned the place into an inviting Christian retreat. Also, he built his own large nursery with a dozen or more separate buildings — using the most advanced technology in the business.

All over his land, Chris built Swiss chalets among the trees. And when Dennis and I were asked to speak for a week's seminar there, we readily agreed.

Ari and Shira, my son-in-law and daughter, and their two children were in America and in the area. I urged them to drop by and visit with us for a day or two at the retreat. Shira said they absolutely had no time, but I kept insisting.

Sure enough, they showed up for not just a day, but stayed a week after we left. When Shira phoned me later, she said, "Mother, these people are not for real." I wondered what her problem was. Then she explained, "They are too godly. We have never met anybody like the Dornbierers."

Today, whenever we have an "excuse" to drop in at the retreat for a day or more, we do so. One of my very favorite places to relax and get quiet before the Lord is there at Blue Mountain Christian Retreat.

Friends help in times of need, and we have many who have done just that. People like Benny Hinn, Jack Hayford, Pat Robertson, Oral Roberts, Jessie Duplantis, Joyce Meyers and Ken Copeland who, though they have heavy financial burdens with their own worldwide ministries, have sowed financially into ours when we've undertaken a new project.

During the *Voice of Healing* days, we made wonderful friends, too. Many have gone to their reward. Those living are still our friends today, such as T.L. Osborn, Walter Kronberg, David Nunn, Kenneth Hagin, John Osteen and Rudy Cerullo.

We continue to make new friends. John Stocker of Resurrection Fellowship in Loveland, Colorado was our commencement speaker in December 1995, when his daughter and her husband both graduated. To our great surprise, he brought with him a check for $50,000 for the renovation of Courts of Praise! (The newlyweds are now youth pastors in a large Dallas church.)

It was really Clinton Utterbach, pastor of Redeeming Love Christian Center in Nanuet, New York, who with his wife, Sarah, got the ball rolling. They were our guest speakers for a week, and after seeing Courts of

Praise, they decided to sow a seed into CFNI. At the end of that week, they presented us with a $25,000 check.

Through the 48 years since the Lord raised up Christ For The Nations (the same year Israel was born), it has really been the small donors who have helped this work continue to move forward. We thank *all* of our friends — and the Lord — from the very depths of our hearts. God bless each one!

And we thank Claude Keeland, who was for many years the president and owner of the bank across the street from our campus. It was he who encouraged and advised us in financial matters after Gordon's death; he assisted us until we could get on a sound monetary basis. He is our dear friend to this day.

"A friend loves at all times, and a brother is born for adversity" (Prov. 17:17).

Chapter Forty-Three

A Genuine Missionary

What qualities does a man called by God need to have to be a missionary? First, he must have a deep experience of salvation and be filled with the Holy Spirit. He must be willing to leave relatives behind; sometimes even his wife and children for a short time. He must integrate into the every culture to which God sends him, without compromise. He must definitely learn the language. He must share what he has generously with those to whom he is ministering. His love for souls must radiate from his countenance. His patience must be self-evident. His prayer life must be consistent. His daily reading, study and preaching of God's Word must be his example. He must be a man above reproach, a man of integrity.

Wayne Myers — and his lovely wife, Martha — is that kind of a missionary. Wayne and Martha became friends of ours shortly before Gordon went to heaven in 1973. Wayne had been a big help in launching our Native Church program. By 1973, we had assisted in building just over 2,000 churches in foreign lands. But with all the financial obligations on hand and no funds, how could we possibly continue the Native Church program?

Wayne and Martha constantly undergirded me. They rented a two bedroom apartment on our campus and used it as the base from which they traveled over the world. We would keep in close contact that way.

We are nearing the 10,000 mark of Native Churches we have helped to build through our faithful donors. The Myers have supervised the building of over 3,500 of those in Mexico. God has provided.

"He who sows sparingly will also reap sparingly, and he who sows bountifully will also reap bountifully" (II Cor. 9:6).

Chapter Forty-Four

Who Despised the Day of Small Things?

Had it not been for Jack Moore of Shreveport, Louisiana, Christ For The Nations might never have started.

When Gordon first began preaching at age 19, he always selected two young men to accompany him: to lead worship, to pray and to preach. To transport the trio, Gordon supplied an old klunk of a car that continually needed repairs. They would evangelize up and down the West Coast and into the Southern states.

It was in Shreveport that Gordon first met Jack, who was the son-in-law of the pastor for whom the trio was holding a revival meeting. Jack was a carpenter and gradually became one of the city's top home contractors. Eventually, Jack became a pastor in Shreveport while building houses one hundred at a time.

Gordon and Jack were intellectuals — both readers and continual students, so they had a lot in common. Besides, when Gordon's trio came through Shreveport, Brother Jack, as everyone lovingly called him, and his wife Mildred, always had a place for them to stay with plenty to eat. This was a bonanza for the fellows, as they were usually hungry with little money for food.

We were pastoring in Ashland, Oregon in 1947 when a knock came on the door. There stood Jack Moore, Gordon's friend, whom I had never met. He told us he had just come from Sacramento where his friend, the Baptist evangelist, William Branham, was preaching. He invited us to accompany him to Sacramento the next day. We accepted.

We arrived in the middle of the day, and lo and behold, to our great surprise, the church was packed — on a weekday! We stayed several days, and by the time we left, Gordon had decided to resign as pastor from our Ashland church. He would join Jack Moore, who was helping line up meetings for Branham as well as preaching.

Meetings followed in Vancouver, B.C.; Tacoma, Washington; Portland, Oregon; and other western cities. Many thousands attended and were getting saved and healed.

By now, Gordon the writer had concluded that a magazine was imperative to carry the Good News all over the world. But an office and funds would be needed. Gordon had neither.

Jack came to the rescue! "Come to Shreveport." So we moved there with our three children. Jack supplied a place to live and an office in the attic above his contracting facility.

His eldest daughter, Anne Jeanne, now a grown-up beautiful young woman with a brilliant mind, became Gordon's assistant editor. I was the secretary who answered the mail and did the proofreading. Both Anna

Jeanne and I worked without a salary. (Gordon's highest salary was $867 a month — in 1973 — and he was driving a 1969 car.)

After three years in Shreveport, Gordon felt we should be located in a larger, more central city. So Jack moved us and built our first office in Dallas.

Jack and Gordon were the best of friends. No doubt, they are continuing that friendship in heaven. We named our lovely library chapel after Jack Moore.

Anna Jeanne is one of the most talented pianists in America. She watches for exceptional students on our campus to encourage and train them. She and I are very close. God had provided the friends we needed.

"Ointment and perfume delight the heart, and the sweetness of a man's friend *gives delight* by hearty counsel" (Prov. 27:9).

Chapter Forty-Five

The Right Employee

Recently, a well-known speaker said, "I lost two years of my ministry by placing a man in a top position he wasn't qualified to fill."

Gordon used to say. "It's a whole lot easier to *hire* an employee in the Lord's work than to fire him. For no matter how poorly he does his job, he'll always have some friends in the organization who will defend him. One of the most difficult jobs I have is selecting a qualified person for each job. A poor, unqualified employee will cost several times what a skilled one would. Choose employees carefully and prayerfully."

The Bible says, "The sons of Issachar ... had understanding of the times, to know what Israel ought to do" (I Chron. 12:32).

God specifically calls businessmen and women when He needs them for the Kingdom. Speaking of Bezelel, the Lord said, "I have filled him with the Spirit of God, in wisdom, in understanding, in knowledge, and in all *manner* of workmanship, to design artistic works, to work in gold, in silver, in bronze, in cutting jewels for setting, in carving wood, and to work all *manner* of workmanship. ... Gifted artisans" (Ex. 31:3-6). God wanted the tabernacle well-built and beautiful.

Once we started the institute, Gordon didn't have time to handle the business matters. Also, he did not feel he was particularly qualified to handle them, and he thought they were too heavy for me.

Shortly before his death, Gordon said to me, "Call Norman."

I asked, "Norman who?"

"The one who married your niece, Linda."

I replied, "If you're thinking of inviting him to work here at CFN, forget it. He's happy in Portland. Both of their parents live there and are getting up in years. Norman has a good job as vice president of the second largest bank in Portland. He and Linda are very active in the Foursquare Church. Linda's sister lives there, too; she has a good job and besides, she doesn't like Dallas."

I figured that would convince Gordon, but it didn't. Without arguing, he simply said, "Call Norman."

I complied and called Norman, and Gordon invited him to fly to Dallas. Norman immediately suspected the true purpose for the invitation, but answered, "I need to check on some land our bank owns near Fort Worth, so I'll be flying there in two weeks. I'll plan to stop by and see you then."

Norman spent that weekend with us as promised. After Gordon invited him to become our business administrator, he answered, "I really can't." Then he gave the same reasons I'd already mentioned to Gordon. I saw the look of disappointment on Gordon's face. He slapped Norman on the shoulder and said, "Norman, if anything ever happens to me, Freda will need you."

Norman replied, "Oh, you'll be here for a long time, won't you?" With that, he departed.

In a few weeks, Gordon went to his eternal reward. Norman and Linda came for the funeral.

Several months later, they did move to Dallas to help us. Norm's expertise in real estate, construction, appraisal, management, and Linda's ability as a top-notch secretary were invaluable to us. My daughter, Shira, cautioned, "Mom, don't expect him to operate like a preacher, which he's not. He's a businessman and will go over everything with a fine-tooth comb." And he did!

For the next 14 years, we saw enormous growth at CFN, both in our school, our campus and also our overseas ministries of Native Churches, literature, Bible schools, etc. Norman operated the ministry on a cash or short-term loan basis. As CFNI grew, we'd need another dormitory. So he and I would negotiate with the owners of adjacent apartments — and there were several from which to choose. We'd purchase one that was priced the best, pay for it and move on to the next.

Norman and Linda traveled with me all over the world, visiting Third-World nations and disaster areas to keep abreast of needs for ministry as well as needs for food, clothing, literature, etc.

After many years, Norman and Linda returned to Portland, which was a great loss, especially to me. But eventually, I saw the hand of God in it all, as both Norman and Linda were able to be with their fathers, who both went to be with the Lord after lingering illnesses.

Norman, who always had a big heart and loved missions, began to find ways to ship donated food, clothing and other supplies overseas. All he needed were funds for the shipping costs. We saw what an enormous benefit this could be to our overseas Bible schools, Native Churches and graduates. So for the last several years, together again, we've teamed up and been able to send literally millions of dollars worth of supplies to the needy — including a beautiful ambulance we together presented to the hospitals in Minsk that treat the Chernobyl children. Likewise, we helped erect the first powdered-milk plant in an uncontaminated area in Belarus.

And here, too, at CFN, God has always supplied. Most recently, he has supplied Mark Ott, a young man who first came to Dallas to attend CFNI 23 years ago. He served in several business positions in our institute, then ventured out on his own, though he kept up his association with CFN. Mark owns a couple of businesses, including a catering business from which he has catered our cafeteria food for several years. Mark has been a teacher at CFNI all these years, a faithful husband and a father of two college students. He is now also our business administrator. Yes, God does provide!

"And whatever you do, do it heartily, as to the Lord and not to men" (Col. 3:23).

Chapter Forty-Six

Not Everybody Likes Me

Victor Richards and his wife were Church of Christ missionaries to Mexico. They had been there for several years holding meetings in their home. Only a few people were coming, and they were discouraged and worn out.

Someone suggested they attend CFN's seminar in Dallas for rest and refreshing. In the early days of our seminars, we would invite active missionaries and their families to come free of charge. We'd give them their meals and housing.

So the Richards decided, "How can we lose?" But when they walked into the auditorium their first night on campus, lo and behold, there was a woman on the platform speaking. They knew from their church dogma that no woman should speak in church. But worse yet, she was taking an offering!

Victor Richards had just about decided to leave the service and go back to their room, when suddenly he actually started listening to the woman. The longer he listened, the more interested he became. By this time, he had concluded that though he was nearly broke, he'd give $25 in the offering. Then he thought, "I'll leave it to my wife. She's generally more generous and may even pledge $100."

To his surprise when he asked her, she replied, "I'll leave it up to you."

"You mean that?"

"Yes," she answered him.

Up went his hand for a $1,000 pledge over the coming year! He could hardly believe what he had done. But the couple stayed for the entire seminar and said they enjoyed it.

They returned to Mexico, and a few days later received a check for $2,400 — the largest they had ever received. They immediately paid their pledge in full, rented a building for their meetings, and began to grow as they moved forward in faith. When an unusually heavy snowstorm caved in their 3,500-seat church roof, Victor built an even bigger edifice with the insurance money!

Then I was invited to speak in that church for their women's conference. Ladies drove hundreds of miles from all over Mexico to get there. It was one of the most fruitful conventions I was ever privileged to address.

By the way, did you guess it? I was the woman on the platform at the Dallas seminar that the Richards didn't like. We're now friends!

Another incident that happened a few years ago was more than a little strange. Perhaps no Bible school is more supportive of Israel than Christ For The Nations Institute. It started that way. Once, when Gordon was accused of being too pro-Israel, his reply was, "I'm pro-Bible." Then he added, "God gave the Jewish people the Word of God through the Old Testament.

Thanks to them, it has been preserved for us. But read the last verse of the Old Testament. It ends with a curse. The Jews should have turned to the next page to see who lifted the curse — Jesus, their Messiah."

One afternoon when some of our students working for our maintenance department were cleaning the auditorium, a woman walked in mumbling aloud to herself. A couple of the students, thinking she was in need, approached her.

She suddenly began to scream out, "Freda Lindsay is a Jew and we're going to kill her!" With that, she ran from the building with such speed, the students, as they watched, declared, "No woman could have run that fast." I've lived on campus with the students for 24 years, and like Gordon used to say, "Up to now, it's worked." Praise God for His protection!

"The LORD redeems the soul of His servants, and none of those who trust in Him shall be condemned" (Psa. 34:22).

Chapter Forty-Seven

Honors Galore!

I recall the night I graduated from high school. That semester, out of a school of 2,000, two scholarships were presented to the "most deserving" young man and woman graduates. Probably because I had worked my way through those four years of school, the teachers selected me as the girl.

Neither my mother nor my father were present, nor were my brothers and sisters. A couple, distant relatives, drove me to and from the graduation exercises. I did have a nice dress for the occasion because for one month before graduation I had worked as an extra at a large department store.

That fall, when others of my classmates started college, I was depressed because my scholarship was only partial, and I had no funds to pay the remainder. Unemployment was high. The only work available was a job as a domestic in a wealthy home. Six weeks passed, and things looked bleaker day by day. Life was drab.

I visited an older sister on Sunday, October 16 (my day off). She suggested, "Why don't you go hear the young evangelist, Gordon Lindsay?"

I told her, "I'm not interested." But I did remember where she said he'd be speaking. As God would have it,

I did attend that service that night — the last one of his campaign. After the benediction, I went to the altar, depressed and under conviction.

As I faced my options — serving God or Satan — there was a real struggle within. Satan, the father of all lies asked: "Do you want to be a wallflower — someone who is always shunned and rejected? How many Christian young people do you know?" (Not many, I confessed.) "You will never have any friends. Don't you want to travel? You will never go anywhere." (I had been to the beach a hundred miles away only once.)

But God also presented His case: "Your sins will all be washed away. You will have peace, protection and eternal life." That night I chose to follow the Lord.

Since then, I have traveled around the world speaking in many nations. I have met world leaders such as President Ronald Reagan, Prime Minister of Israel Yitzhak Shamir, Prime Minister of India Indira Ghandi, President of Guatemala Efrin Rios-Montt, senators and congressmen of every variety, etc. Plus thousands of ministers, including Dr. Cho of Seoul, Korea, pastor of the world's largest church. (Christ For The Nations helped him build his first church.)

At the luxurious home of former owner of the Dallas Cowboys, Clint Murchison, I was honored as Christian Woman of the Year in 1983, with many friends present at the gala event. Dr. Cory SerVaas of the *Saturday Evening Post* and Anne Murchison presented me with the award.

The late Dr. David du Plessis of South Africa was very close to Gordon and me. It was he who "crossed over" to meet with the mainline Protestants and Catholics to encourage them to move into the flow of the Spirit, which many did.

Dr. du Plessis had his office on our campus for three years, with CFN giving him the financial support necessary. Later, he was honored in Pasadena, California at Fuller Theological Seminary, where a library with his personal memoirs was dedicated to him. I was invited and attended the dedication.

I've been on virtually every national Christian TV station, as well as in Canada, plus many local ones along with interviews on radio, including my own radio program for several years.

My alma mater, LIFE College of the Foursquare Gospel, honored me with a doctorate of divinity. Oral Roberts University honored me with a doctorate of humane letters.

Probably my greatest honor was when I was asked to speak at the Washington For Jesus Rally with a half a million present. "Were you nervous?" I've been asked.

My answer, "It's easier to speak to a large crowd than to a small one. Because in a small audience you're so close you look right into their faces."

The internationally-known evangelist Benny Hinn happened to be holding services in Dallas about the time of my 80th birthday. He called me to the pulpit and had the 12,000 people sing *Happy Birthday* to me. Quite exciting!

I counted it a great honor when I was asked to speak in Springfield, Missouri at the Signs and Wonders Conference for the Assemblies of God with about 1,800 pastors and workers present.

Who would ever have believed that this little girl, born of poor immigrant parents in a sod house, one of twelve brothers and sisters, who didn't know a word of English when starting the first grade, could ever be blessed of the Lord and so honored? Praise God!

"He has put down the mighty from *their* thrones, and exalted *the* lowly" (Lk. 1:52).

Chapter Forty-Eight

A 55-Year-Long Prayer

In our walk with the Lord, there will be times that before we even pray, God has already answered. "It shall come to pass that before they call, I will answer; and while they are still speaking, I will hear" (Isa. 65:24). That's God's Word.

At other times, the waiting period is prolonged. In some cases, it seems an eternity.

In my family there were eight girls. Edith was three years younger than I and was also born in a sod house in Canada.

When she was about 19, she worked nights at a restaurant in Portland, Oregon. One of the customers, Alan, offered to drive her home after work rather than see her ride the streetcar each night. Unable to attend church regularly because of her employment, Edith lost out with God. Alan also came from a Christian family, but declared himself an atheist. Soon the two were married.

During their lives together, they never attended church, prayed, nor did they teach their son the Word. Many years later, when Alan was on his deathbed with cancer, he prayed the sinner's prayer and said he was ready to meet God.

After Alan died, Edith still refused to go to church or have any fellowship with Christians. For 55 years, we sisters had been praying for her.

Then I heard that the Assemblies of God were having their 44th General Council in Portland. I felt this was the time to reach Edith, so I flew to Portland and stayed with my youngest sister, Elma.

Immediately upon arrival, I phoned Edith to ask her to go with us the next night to the opening of the conference. "Oh, Freda, you know I don't go to church. I don't have a decent dress to wear. I have my grandson to take care of." On and on, she made one excuse after another. But this time, I was determined to take her if I had to literally pick her up and carry her.

To my pleasant surprise, she came to spend the following day with Elma and me. Yes, she did bring along her "good" dress, and yes, she did go to the opening service with us.

The auditorium was packed. The choir and music were phenomenal. The message was powerful!

An "inventory" card was passed to each person for self-examination purposes to pinpoint their standing with God — both now and for the future. A place for a signature was also included.

When the glorious service had ended, Elma and I held the cards in our hands without signing them. Edith leaned over to me and asked for a pencil, which I gave her. She signed her name on the card and prayed the sinner's prayer with the evangelist.

The transformation was amazing! Since that time, Edith has faithfully attended church, and she loves it.

When she visited me here in Dallas for the first time, the first thing she said after she hugged me was, "Freda, I'm a real Christian now."

After 55 years of praying daily for her, God answered our prayers! It was worth it!

"Cast your bread upon the waters, for you will find it after many days" (Eccl. 11:1).

Chapter Forty-Nine

Crossing Over

For too long, we have built high walls, or at least fences, around "our territory." This seems to be true of every church organization. There are various reasons: Sometimes, a fear of rejection, a feeling that we alone have the whole truth, fear that some other ministry might get some of our members or some of our finances, worry that we might receive criticism from the organization officials, and on and on.

For years Gordon was friends with Dr. W.A. Criswell, the prominent pastor of the First Baptist Church in Dallas, of which Billy Graham is a member. Anne Criswell, his daughter, worked for a short period of time in our print shop and became acquainted with our daughter Carole (Shira). Anne has a beautiful voice and Carole is an accomplished pianist, so the two would on occasion team up. But publicly our families stayed "safe distances."

For each commencement here at CFNI, we look for an outstanding speaker. Usually, a list is given to me to help make the final choice. One semester when the then academic dean, Dr. Eric Belcher, brought me a list, the number one recommendation read: Dr. W.A. Criswell.

Returning the list, I said, "Count him as one chance

in a hundred of accepting." And I glanced at the other names without further comment. As he left my office, I suggested, "Make that one in a thousand!"

A couple of weeks later, Dr. Belcher walked into my office, wearing a slight smile and a pleased look on his face. Without saying a word, he handed me a letter. It read, "I'll be happy to be your commencement speaker." It was signed, "W.A. Criswell." We both broke out in a praise to the Lord, and I had to eat "humble pie" for my incorrect prediction.

Dr. Criswell did come. Our 2,200 seat auditorium was filled, our students welcomed him with a standing ovation both before and after he preached. He told the students, "I wish the Baptists would sing like you do." Then he spoke without notes like a man from another world! Afterward, he left hurriedly to speak at another appointment — the fourth for the day!

One of the graduates told me later at the reception, "If Dr. Criswell had invited everyone to come forward who needed God, no doubt the whole graduating class would have been at the altar."

I quipped, "Oh, thank the Lord he didn't. The audience would have concluded we are graduating a class of sinners!"

Several days later, I received a beautiful letter from Dr. Criswell in which he modestly wrote, "It was one of the highlights of my life — speaking at your school." ... Bless him, Lord!

"How could one have chased 1,000 and two put 10,000 to flight, except their rock had sold them, and the Lord had delivered them up?" (Deut. 32:30 AMP).

Chapter Fifty

My Greatest Joy

God blessed Gordon and me with three healthy children for which I praise Him. All three are different from one another. All graduated from different universities.

Shira, the oldest, has a call to Israel where she has labored with Ari, her husband, for 28 years, working with messianic Jews, among other things. (See chapter eight.) They have a son, Ayal, and a daughter, Shani.

Dennis, the youngest, married Ginger in 1970 after graduating from Southern California College. Together they served with Youth With A Mission for four years including attending its School of Evangelism and L'Abri Fellowship. When Gordon died in 1973, Dennis and Ginger moved to Dallas. Since that time, Dennis has taught at CFNI. He developed a special interest in creation science and is finishing his eleventh book on the subject. He is now President, CEO and Chairman of the Board of Christ For The Nations.

Dennis and Ginger have three children: Missy, Hawni and Golan. In the last few years, Ginger has begun hosting an annual women's conference, which has been a tremendous blessing.

Gilbert, a graduate of Baylor University with a business major, chose printing as his profession. He and his wife, Shirley, have three children: Michael, Julia and Marcy.

I had prayed even before the birth of our three, that all would be "in the ministry." So when Gil took over our small printing plant after graduating from college, I was sure this was to be only a "temporary" job. I was waiting for God to make a preacher out of him. But more and more he became involved in printing.

One day, I asked God, "What's spiritual about printing?" True, Gil printed ours and several other Christian magazines, gospel books, tracts, etc. But anybody could do that. I quite regularly complained to God.

About five years ago, Gilbert came to me one day saying, "Mom, you know Russia is opening up. A number of businessmen are going into an operation called Joint Ventures, where an American joins up with a Russian partner."

My response was immediate, "Oh, son, you can't trust the communists! Beware!"

To make a long story short, Gilbert did go to Belarus and rented printing space from the Communist Academy of Science, which had printed much of Russia's propaganda and books.

In the last several years, Gilbert has printed multiplied millions of Bibles, New Testaments and gospel books in not only Russian, but also for the former Eastern Bloc nations. These are being produced for major ministries from the United States, Scandinavia and other European countries.

Has it been easy? Gil says, "For every book and Bible

that comes off the press, I have to fight the demons of hell." But God has given him the victory in spite of three trials that went to Russia's Supreme Court — all of which he won; government taxes in one year that cost him $100,000 (U.S.), shut downs while electricity in the plant was deliberately turned off for two weeks, and he had to pay the 160 employees full wages.

But like I told Dennis and Shira one day, "You know, Gilbert is doing more to reach the lost for Christ, than all the rest of our family put together." So all of my family is in the ministry!

I had to apologize to God.

And all eight grandchildren are serving the Lord — four in college, three in high school and Michael, the oldest, helping his father now in the printing business.

All different talents — one is a singer, another is a pianist, one is gifted in sports, another is a secretary and Michael is in business.

So, my greatest joy? To see my children, their spouses and my eight grandchildren all saved, filled with the Holy Spirit and serving God.

He has indeed provided for every situation!

To God be all the glory!

"Train up a child in the way he should go, and when he is old he will not depart from it" (Prov. 22:6).

Like my dear friend, missionary Esther Marocco, once said to me when she felt I should give a little more time to my family: "What shall it profit a woman if she gains (or wins) the whole world and loses her own children and grandchildren?"

I remember once when Gordon came home from an

overseas trip, he brought me a plaque which reads: "As for me and my house, we will serve the LORD" (Josh. 24:15). I hung it on the wall above the kitchen table, where my children would see it each day while eating their breakfast. It worked!

So God's plan — Providential Promised Provision Provided — has worked in my own life and that of Christ For The Nations in its 48-year history. To Him be the glory!

Experience.

There's no substitute for it. Experience is the accumulation of tests and answered and unanswered prayer which together produce wisdom, character and great faith. In her revealing book, *My Diary Secrets*, Mrs. Gordon Lindsay remembers her walk of faith; her courtship and marriage to Gordon, one of America's most beloved evangelists, authors and teachers; and their life of ministry. Together they founded Christ For The Nations, a missionary-service organization that reaches around the world; and Christ For The Nations Institute, a two-year Bible school in Dallas, Texas, that has grown beyond anyone's expectations since its establishment in 1970.

My Diary Secrets is a candid view of their ministry, its disappointments and joys, a remarkable, unforgettable story of God's mighty anointing on a young Spirit-filled couple as they devoted their lives to His service.

$4.95

Please add $1 for postage and handling.

ORDER FROM:
CFN Books
P.O. Box 769000
Dallas, TX 75376-9000
Phone: (214) 376-1711

SPECIAL NOTE: A free gift subscription to CHRIST FOR THE NATIONS magazine is available to those who write to Christ For The Nations, P.O. Box 769000, Dallas, TX 75376-9000. This magazine contains special feature stories of men of faith and includes prophetic articles on the latest world developments. Why not include the names of your friends? (Due to high mailing rates, this applies only to Canada and the U.S.)

Sequel to *My Diary Secrets*

Freda Lindsay's life journey has brought her from the obscure sod house of her birth on the windswept plains of Saskatchewan, Canada to a worldwide renowned ministry.

In her book *My Diary Secrets*, Freda Lindsay gave readers an intimate look into her childhood years and marriage to evangelist Gordon Lindsay and their ministry together. Now in the sequel, *Freda: The Widow Who Took Up the Mantle*, Freda continues her chronicle of God's intervention in her life.

Be inspired and built-up in faith as you read about a woman of strength, courage and vision — Freda Lindsay.

$4.95

Please add $1 for postage and handling.

Order from:
CFN Books • P.O. Box 769000
Dallas, TX 75376-9000
Phone: (214) 376-1711

The ABCs for Godly Living
by Freda Lindsay

A GREAT GIFT FOR ANYONE, ANYTIME!

Not just for children — parents and grandparents will benefit, too. Freda Lindsay's book covers major biblical subjects such as salvation, healing, love, discipline, the Holy Spirit and others.

$8.95

Please add $1 for postage and handling.

Order from:
CFN Books • P.O. Box 769000 • Dallas, TX 75376-9000
(214) 376-1711